KU-059-529

*Reformation*
# WOMEN

# *Reformation* WOMEN

## Sixteenth-Century Figures Who Shaped Christianity's Rebirth

Rebecca VanDoodewaard

An updated text based on James I. Good's
*Famous Women of the Reformed Church*

**Reformation Heritage Books**
Grand Rapids, Michigan

*Reformation Women*
© 2017 by Rebecca VanDoodewaard

All rights reserved. No part of this book may be used or reproduced in any manner whatsoever without written permission except in the case of brief quotations embodied in critical articles and reviews. Direct your requests to the publisher at the following addresses:

**Reformation Heritage Books**
2965 Leonard St. NE
Grand Rapids, MI 49525
616–977–0889 / Fax 616–285–3246
orders@heritagebooks.org
www.heritagebooks.org

Scripture taken from the New King James Version®. Copyright © 1982 by Thomas Nelson. Used by permission. All rights reserved.

*Printed in the United States of America*
17 18 19 20 21 22/10 9 8 7 6 5 4 3 2 1

Library of Congress Cataloging-in-Publication Data

Names: VanDoodewaard, Rebecca, author.
Title: Reformation women : sixteenth-century figures who shaped Christianity's
   rebirth / Rebecca VanDoodewaard.
Description: Grand Rapids, Michigan : Reformation Heritage Books, 2017.
   | "An updated text based on James I. Good's Famous women of the
   Reformed Church." | Includes bibliographical references and index.
Identifiers: LCCN 2017006598 | ISBN 9781601785329 (pbk. : alk. paper)
Subjects: LCSH: Reformed Church—Biography. | Women in church work—
   Reformed Church. | Church history—16th century.
Classification: LCC BX9417 .V36 2017 | DDC 284/.209252 [B]—dc23 LC
   record available at https://lccn.loc.gov/2017006598

*For additional Reformed literature, request a free book list from Reformation Heritage Books at the above regular or e-mail address.*

*For my mother and grandmothers,*

who between them survived war, poverty, and new places,
raised orphans, educate children,
visited those in prison, care for the dying,
give generously to those in need,
wash the feet of the saints,
and pray for Reformation.

*We know that man was not created or regenerated through faith in order to be idle, but rather that without ceasing he should do those things which are good and useful. For in the Gospel the Lord says that a good tree brings forth good fruit (Matt. 12:33), and that he who abides in me bears much fruit (John 15:5).*
—Second Helvetic Confession, 1566

# CONTENTS

# PREFACE

What would Luther have been without his Katie? At best, he would have trudged along with his work, sleeping alone and depressed in the stinking sheets that he later described in a letter.[1] With his wife, he was energized, encouraged, and clean; he was able to better connect with other people, maintain his health, get feedback on his writing, and enjoy a pleasant home. Katie facilitated and furthered the Reformation.

Women are an essential element in church history. Just as Sarah, Deborah, Esther, and the New Testament Marys helped shape Bible history, so the women of the Reformed church have helped to make its history great. "Wherever true Christianity has emerged," writes one historian, "there women have been found to pour their early and willing tribute."[2] Often, as in the New Testament, it is the women who believe first and serve sacrificially. History bears this out repeatedly. Jeanne d'Albret, one of the queens in this book, once wrote, "If I wished to take the defense of my sex, I could find plenty of examples." People who ignore or belittle the role of women, she asserted, "deserve only pity... for their ignorance."[3] Biblical Christianity values

---

1. Luther's work kept him busy, and clean sheets were not a priority; he slept in one unwashed set for more than a year until they were "foul with sweat." As quoted in Roland Bainton, *Here I Stand* (New York: Abingdon Press, 1950), 290.

2. Caroline Bowles, *Olympia Morata: Her Times, Life, and Writings, Arranged from Contemporary and Other Authorities* (London: Smith, Elder and Co., 1834), xiii.

3. Quoted in Nancy Lyman Roelker, *Queen of Navarre: Jeanne d'Albret, 1528–1572* (Cambridge, Mass.: Harvard University Press, 1968), 421.

women and their contributions to Christ's church and society. Certainly our understanding of church history and women's potential fruitfulness will be much richer when we get to know these examples. There are three main reasons that the church today needs to meet these women and follow their examples.

First, women make up roughly half of a population, including Europe's Protestant population in the sixteenth century. And the women of that day were not just sitting around waiting for their husbands to do things: they were reading, writing, and ruling. They were teaching children, sheltering refugees, and balancing husbands. They directed armies, confronted kings, and rebuked heretics. Limiting our study of Reformation history to men limits us to half a history. Unless we understand at least some of these women's work and influence, we will have an incomplete picture of God's work during this century.

Second, feminist historians are interested in women's history. The University of Chicago Press has reflected this interest by publishing a series of the works of early modern women, including several Protestant women.[4] While it is wonderful to have primary sources in modern English, feminist historians are casting these Christians as protofeminists. Marriages in which husbands respected their wives' intellectual abilities and churches that appreciated female gifts are presented as exceptions to the Reformed rule, when they are simply sample expressions of a widespread biblical complementarianism during the Reformation, as many of the marriages in this book show. Feminist reinterpretations of these women's lives and work are damaging the witness that these Christians left us. The church needs to retake its territory here.

The third reason the study of Reformation women is important is because the church is struggling to rightly understand and express biblical womanhood. We tend to think of our own time— this era of church history—as unique in its problem of sorting out women's roles. Different churches and denominations have different

---

4. Publication began in 1996; the series covers a wide range of figures.

approaches, but even for groups that are complementarian, there can be large differences and disagreements. But the church has dealt with this matter before: the Reformation was a period of huge social adjustment as Roman Catholic tradition dealing with women's roles fell apart under scriptural examination. Runaway nuns, female mystics, and powerful Roman Catholic queens revealed real issues confronting early Protestantism. As the church developed a biblical understanding of womanhood, Protestant women lived out the full scope and power of that womanhood. A range of personalities, abilities, and positions gives us a sample spectrum of what faithful, strong service to Christ and His church looked like then. These same principles and examples are invaluable for helping women today bear fruit within the broad boundaries that God gives us in His Word.

The subjects of this book are limited to women who are not household names in modern evangelicalism. Today, many Christian women are familiar with figures like Lady Jane Grey, but few know about Louise de Coligny. One of the goals of this book is to introduce today's Christians to believing women who helped form our Reformed faith but who are largely unknown now. Biographies of women like Katharine Luther are available, but biographies of equally influential and godly women are not, and the church needs them; these women form a large section in the cloud of witnesses.[5] Women from this seminal century of Protestantism have much to teach us.

Germany, France, and England give us the largest number of Reformation women. Other countries did have their Reformers and female martyrs—even countries like Spain saw women convert out of Roman Catholicism—but their influence often died with them.[6] Some areas of Europe, like Scandinavia, had Protestant queens or

---

5. An excellent biography of Katharine Luther is Ernst Kroker, *The Mother of the Reformation: The Amazing Life and Story of Katharine Luther*, trans. Mark E. DeGarmeaux (St. Louis: Concordia, 2013).

6. Roland Bainton's volume *Women of the Reformation: From Spain to Scandinavia* (Minneapolis: Augsburg, 1977), illustrates the paucity of strong, Reformed figures available and the lack of information on the women whom we do know existed.

noblewomen, but there is not enough available information about their lives or work to include them in this collection. The countries where the Reformation had a strong, Calvinist influence and an established Protestant church left the greatest record of influential women, so three countries contribute most of the figures.[7] Because England's Reformed women, like Jane Grey, are better known, Britain's contribution in this volume is limited to Katherine Willoughby.[8]

Many of the women in this book came from noble or royal families. Those who did not had famous husbands who brought them along into recorded history. The disproportionate number of noble and royal women compared with commoners simply results from the lack of literacy and influence that the lower classes—especially women—had in the sixteenth century. No doubt there were women who furthered the Reformation about whom we do not know because they did not have the ability or time to leave records of their lives.

Despite often being rich or royal, these women are a diverse group, with different personalities, nationalities, abilities, and family backgrounds. Many began life wealthy; some were poor. Some did what they were raised to do; for others, rebellion against their upbringing was the beginning of faithfulness. Many had wonderful marriages; others suffered because of their husbands. One was single. Some died old and full of years while a few died young. But several characteristics are common to all these believing women.

---

7. Reformation women in the Netherlands were usually German or French princesses and are not considered here as products of the Dutch Reformation, though they contributed to it.

8. For a biography of Jane Grey, see Faith Cook, *Lady Jane Grey: Nine Day Queen of England* (Darlington, U.K.: Evangelical Press, 2005). Some evangelicals see Anne Boleyn as a Reformation figure: see, for example, J. H. Merle d'Aubigne, *The Reformation in England* (Edinburgh: Banner of Truth, 1994), 2:191, 263. Although she was at the heart of the events that shifted England away from Roman Catholicism and introduced several Protestant writings to the court and country, there is little evidence that she was converted; Anne spent much time in her last days confessing to Catholic clergy and took the Mass before her execution. Eric Ives, *The Life and Death of Anne Boleyn* (Oxford: Blackwell Publishing, Ltd., 2004), 353–54, 356.

First, they were devoted to the Protestant church. It was the core around which their lives revolved. Sometimes their contributions were direct: issuing edicts, writing theological works, and establishing congregations. Others found themselves in a position to bring reform indirectly by supporting husbands, reviewing book manuscripts, sheltering refugees, and educating children to carry on the work. Regardless of how it was done, they devoted their lives to the establishment and growth of a biblically Reformed church.

Second, if they were married to believers, they were devoted to their husbands' work. Many of these women married men who brought about, shaped, or advanced the Reformation; in supporting them, these wives facilitated the work of preaching and pastoring that they were unable to do themselves.

Third, they were given to hospitality. The level of hospitality these women practiced is almost unheard of in the West today. Groups of orphans, refugees, visiting pastors, and many others crowded their homes and lands; all were fed, clothed, and encouraged. The generosity these women displayed was sacrificial in terms of energy, time, and finances.

Fourth, the women in this book stewarded their intellectual abilities. Some were given excellent educations as children; others were self-taught. All of them worked to understand Scripture and theology, reading, discussing, and corresponding with theologians to do so. This was no ivory tower experience. Instead, education was a means of using God-given intellect in order to bear more fruit. These women also worked to educate younger siblings, children, or orphans in their care; they knew that they were raising the next generation of political and theological leaders and equipped them accordingly.

Last, they were brave. Once they saw the right course of action, they obeyed, even in frightening circumstances. Facing angry monarchs, assassins, persecutions, exile, and other challenges with fortitude seems to have been standard. Some of them may have been princesses, but there were no princess complexes. Real femininity is strength—a uniquely feminine strength that is tough *and* ladylike.

Their unusual deeds stand out to us: fleeing in disguise, preventing war, enduring persecution, and resisting arranged marriages. But
it is often their everyday faithfulness that was most formative for
the church—husbands supported, children taught, saints sheltered,
Bibles read and distributed. Few women today have the opportunity to command an army, but all believing women can be faithful
in the mundane, obeying in their own circumstances. Perhaps that
is the more challenging and daunting call. It is the example of
everyday faithfulness changing families, churches, and nations that
makes these women's stories so valuable for us today.

Originally, most of these chapters were a series of articles written
for a denominational magazine in the late Victorian era. A publisher
later collected the articles and sold them in one volume, *Famous
Women of the Reformed Church*. Author James Isaac Good prefaced
the book with his hope that "the lives of these Reformed saints will
stimulate the ladies of our Church to greater interest in our splendid Church history, and to greater activity as in missions and the
practical work of the Church in which they already excel."[9] Here,
Good's work has been revised, expanded, and corrected to make the
stories of these remarkable women accessible for today's church.[10]
Any unattributed quotes are from his work. Because many of the
women married more than once, I have used their maiden names or
commonly accepted name forms in chapter titles for clarity.[11] Each

---

9. James Isaac Good, preface to *Famous Women of the Reformed Church* (n.p.:
Sunday School Board of the Reformed Church in the United States, 1901).

10. This volume has removed many original chapters and added a chapter on
Katherine Willoughby in order to give readers a more balanced collection of formative
but lesser known individuals from the sixteenth century.

11. Because most of the women in this book were married more than once and
often had titles, various authors use various names. For example, Charlotte, whose
maiden name was Arbaleste, first married a man named de Feuqueres, then one named
de Mornay, but is often referred to in primary sources by her second husband's title,
du Plessis. To complicate things, women in high-ranking families were often related,
so that someone's maiden name could be someone else's first or second married name.
To try to avoid confusion, modern scholars usually identify women by their maiden
names, sometimes hyphenated with married names, or by royal titles.

chapter is a biographical sketch—an introduction to a woman who could be the subject of an entire book. Hopefully, these chapters whet our appetites for more about the female saints who have gone before us.

Several people deserve thanks for their help in producing this volume. My grandmother gave incentive to start when she said that another book project would keep me out of trouble. Laura Ladwig and Kim Dykema at Puritan Reformed Theological Seminary went above and beyond the call of librarian duty, working interlibrary loan wonders. Dr. David Noe kindly translated some Latin; Stephanie MacDonald answered questions about French. Dr. Todd Rester translated the Bucer-Blaurer letters into English. Paige Kamp read the manuscript and had helpful thoughts and criticisms. My parents and sisters gave encouragement, feedback, and design help (thanks, Mary!), and my children sweetly showed interest in another project. Without my husband, this book would not have developed: he gave me Good's book in the first place, brought home other volumes and peanut butter cups, directed me to sources, answered questions about the sixteenth-century church, listened to anecdotes, and for a few months often ate pizza for supper so that these women's stories could become better known. Thank you, Bill!

# INTRODUCTION

The sixteenth century changed Europe and consequently the world. Transformations that came as a consequence of new spiritual clarity touched every aspect of life, from politics to preaching to parenting. Because the chapters of this book focus on specific women exemplifying this change in everyday life, major events, documents, and figures are briefly explained here to provide a larger context.

## Germany and Switzerland

When Martin Luther nailed his Ninety-Five Theses to the door in Wittenberg in 1517, Germany was a collection of dozens of small states and city-states under the oversight of the Holy Roman Emperor, Charles V. Initially all Roman Catholic, a few princes converted to Lutheranism, making it the religion of their regions. Charles V remained Roman Catholic throughout his life, putting the young Protestant church under sustained pressure until 1555, when he legalized Lutheranism with the Peace of Augsburg. Despite sociopolitical conflict that was sometimes expressed in revolt or battle, Luther, along with men like Philip Melanchthon and Martin Bucer, worked to teach, protect, and expand Christ's church throughout the states. Reform was also costly for German princes, personally and politically. One of these, Frederick III, sponsored a local professor to write the Heidelberg Catechism.

South of Germany in Switzerland, Ulrich Zwingli began preaching in 1519. Like Luther, he saw not only corruption but also theological error in the Roman Catholic Church. Reform spread through the Swiss cantons, bringing military conflict and the battle that killed Zwingli. The man who took his place as pastor was Heinrich Bullinger; he authored the Second Helvetic Confession, which became one of the standard documents of the Reformed church in countries throughout Europe.

## France

Ruled by absolute monarchs, France quickly turned against the Reformation, exiling, then executing, people who refused to recant their Protestant faith. John Calvin was one of the exiles. He became a Reformation colossus, shaping Protestantism by his theological works. Either in person or by letter, Calvin was also a friend and counselor to many Protestant women, including royals.

Though several firstborn princesses converted to Protestantism, France's Salic law allowed only men to rule. The only French king who claimed Protestantism was Henry IV, and he renounced Calvinism for Catholicism in a highly political move that grieved his believing sister. Despite that, he did issue the Edict of Nantes in 1598, which gave the French Reformed, or Huguenots, religious liberty that outraged the pope. While the Edict did decriminalize Protestantism, it outlined restrictions on the Huguenot church and confirmed Roman Catholicism as France's official religion.

## England

Henry VIII was an unlikely candidate to bring reform to England. But God used his lust for power, women, and wealth to split with the Church of Rome and make Protestantism England's official religion. For Henry, it was a political move that gave him total power, a male heir, and the confiscated wealth of British monasteries. After Henry's death, his only son, Edward VI, ruled. In six years, Edward's Reformed beliefs changed England's form of worship, promoted evangelical thought, and gave Protestant pastors prominence. Bishops like Thomas Cranmer and Hugh Latimer—true believers who valued the Word— were encouraged to preach and write. England became a safe haven for French, Polish, and other Continental refugees fleeing Roman

Catholic persecution. But Edward died young, and Henry VIII's great niece, the evangelical Lady Jane Grey, succeeded him, ruling for only nine days. Henry's Roman Catholic daughter Mary dragged the country back into medieval Roman Catholicism, executing so many Protestants that she is known as Bloody Mary. When she died a few years later, her half sister, Elizabeth I, ended the persecutions with her long reign of religious moderation.

## Spain and the Netherlands

In the sixteenth century, Roman Catholic Spain was rich and powerful, throwing the weight of its growing empire against the small Protestant church. A few years before Luther began teaching, Spain had finally driven Islam out of its borders and was determined to do the same to the new "heresy." Sometimes it did this through political pressure, strongly pushing marriage or other agreements to keep the balance of power on its side. Sometimes it opposed reform through military confrontation or occupation. Always it used the Inquisition within its borders: intimidating, torturing, and executing to stamp out anything not in line with conservative Roman Catholicism.

The Netherlands was a place that Spain occupied. Philip II of Spain, Bloody Mary's husband and Charles V's son, pushed the Low Countries hard as they turned to Protestantism. High taxation and open persecution were chosen means to break Dutch revolt against Spain's rule. Guido de Bres, a Dutch theologian who wrote the Belgic Confession to explain Protestant beliefs to the Spanish, was one of the martyrs under Spain's occupation. But as so often happened in this time, God turned larger Roman Catholic plans on their head.

William the Silent was a Roman Catholic prince when Charles V made him governor of the Netherlands. Seeing Roman Catholic cruelty made William question Spain's position; by 1580 he had converted to Calvinism and openly declared himself in opposition to Spanish occupation. In the war that followed, William was assassinated. His son Maurice continued the fight against Spain, winning greater independence for the Dutch. During his rule, a synod met at Dordrecht to deal with theological controversy caused by the rise of Arminianism. The document produced by the synod, the Canons of Dort, became a confessional standard throughout much of continental Europe, along with the Belgic Confession and the Heidelberg Catechism.

## Conclusion

Reformation did not come easily to Europe, but the Lord used a group of faithful Christians that was often small and powerless to bring salvation to many people walking in darkness. They faced many obstacles and deprivations, but the Lord gave them pastors who truly loved their people, fellowship with each other that crossed national borders, and the opportunity to read His Word through vernacular translations. Theological divisions existed within Protestantism, sometimes leading to fractured congregations and relationships—even countries—but this did not prevent biblical truth from transforming a continent.

# 1

## Anna Reinhard

At the top of a Swiss lake, Zurich straddles a river. In 1518 it was the economic capital of the Roman Catholic cantons recovering from a series of wars with France, Italy, and other neighbors. That year Ulrich Zwingli arrived in Zurich and took up his duties in the cathedral. Like Calvin's wife, Idelette, Anna Reinhard was a pious widow when her future husband arrived in town as the new priest. Anna's home was not far from the parsonage in Zurich.

We are not sure of Anna's birth year, but it was likely 1484. Her father was a middle-class landlord. We know nothing about her youth, except that she was beautiful and that a young man in town, John von Knonau, wanted to marry her. But John's father had chosen another bride for him. The von Knonau family was among the oldest and most prominent in Zurich. John's father was proud of his family and wanted his son to maintain his position in the aristocracy, so he sent John to the court of the bishop of Konstanz to be educated. While John was there, his father chose an Austrian daughter-in-law of noble birth. But John had already decided. He preferred a Swiss commoner to a foreign noblewoman.

John and Anna secretly married in 1504 at a village chapel in Zurich. When John's father found out, he was furious. He forbade John to enter the house and disinherited him. Anna's husband now had to make his own way. In 1511, he was elected to the city council despite his father's efforts to prevent it, then became an ensign in the Swiss army, going to Italy to fight in the wars against France in an effort to support his family. After several campaigns he returned in broken health and died, leaving Anna a widow with a son and two daughters, one of whom died in infancy.

It was John and Anna's son, Gerold, who brought his mother and Zwingli together. Zwingli came to Zurich late in 1518, when Anna was struggling to support and train her family, hindered by her small income. From the beginning of Zwingli's preaching ministry, she was one of his most attentive listeners. Her home was in his parish, and he came in contact with her as her pastor. He soon saw her needs and Christian graces, but it was Gerold especially who attracted his attention. Zwingli's quick eye saw the boy's talents. He gave him private lessons in Greek and Latin. When Gerold needed higher education at the age of eleven, Zwingli sent him to Basel, Switzerland's literary center. The boy was so bright that his teacher at Basel wrote back to Zwingli, "If you have any more such boys, send them to me."

But whether through pride or another temptation, Gerold fell in with bad company and began to live immorally. In 1523, Zwingli wrote a book for Gerold titled *Directions for the Education of a Young Nobleman* and dedicated it to him, urging him to biblical morals and a Christian life. Apparently, this timely appeal saved the boy. Gerold seems to have been converted and began a new life. Bright and promising, he quickly rose to the highest positions in Zurich despite his age—a member of the city council at eighteen and president of the city council at twenty-one. Zwingli's fatherly care for Gerold opened the way for marriage with the young man's mother. As he shared Anna's concerns for Gerold, Zwingli became more and more concerned with Anna and fell in love with her.

But there were difficulties in the way of the marriage: priests could not marry.[1] The couple feared people's opposition to their marriage and the damage it could have on Zwingli's ministry. So for the second time, Anna was secretly wed, this time to Zwingli, who

---

1. Zwingli wrote a petition to the bishop of Konstanz, asking him to grant permission to priests to marry. It is dated July 2, 1522. Ulrich Zwingli, *The Latin Works and the Correspondence of Huldreich Zwingli Together with Selections from His German Works* (New York: G. P. Putnam's Sons, 1912), 1:150.

kept his marriage hidden from all but his closest friends until 1524. Eventually, news of the marriage caused a great sensation, far beyond Zurich. Zwingli was the first Reformer to marry. The Roman Catholics charged him with breaking his vows and marrying Anna for her beauty and her money. He replied that she was not worth more than four hundred guilders. Perhaps Anna's beauty had played into things; this charge was not so bluntly refuted.

After marrying Zwingli, Anna stopped wearing jewelry. We don't know her reasons. Maybe vanity was a personal vice she fought; maybe she thought it would help the family financially. Perhaps the busyness of her new life crowded out all extras: she was wife to a famous Reformer, cared for the city's poor, visited the sick, bore and raised children, and hosted many in her home. As her husband cared for parish souls, she tried to bring relief in physical trials.

Anna's care for her husband was even greater than her care for the parish. Zwingli called her his dearest housewife, a useful helpmeet in his work. He was a good father to all the children, who loved to hear him play the fiddle.[2] When Zwingli became too absorbed in his work, rising early and working late, she would, as he said in a letter to a friend, pull his sleeve and whisper in his ear, "Take a little more rest, my dear." She loved to hear Zwingli explain an aspect of Christ's character that she had not understood. When her husband, with the other Zurich ministers, began translating the Bible in 1525, he read her the proofs every evening before bed.[3] Anna loved hearing the gospel story in her own tongue. When the complete Bible was published in 1529, Zwingli gave her a copy; it became her favorite book. She tried to make sure that every family in the congregation had a copy at home.

One letter from Zwingli to Anna has survived. It was written from Berne in 1528, when Anna gave birth in his absence. In it, he

---

2. Roland Bainton, *Women of the Reformation in Germany and Italy* (Minneapolis, Minn.: Augsburg, 1971), 162.

3. It was finished several years before Luther's complete Bible appeared in 1534; like Anna, Katharine Luther also listened to or read through proofs in the evening when her domestic work was finished.

thanks the Lord for the arrival of a son, praying that both parents might be able to educate him well; urges Anna not to be anxious about his safety; and sends greetings to friends.

Anna welcomed large numbers of her husband's friends and entertained his guests. There were many Protestant refugees in those days, and Zwingli's house was always open to them. When Zwingli was engaged or away, Anna was the center of the circle. Leading citizens and ministers like Leo Juda, Pellican, and others gave her great credit and praise. The upper chancellor of Silesia visited in 1526 and was so impressed by Zwingli's home that he declared he would never forget it and called Anna an "angel wife."

But married life had care as well as honor. Zwingli lived in continual danger of assassination or kidnapping by Roman Catholics, and it concerned Anna. He could not go out alone after dark and had to be careful where he ate or drank for fear of poisoning. If she noticed any danger, Anna called for help. When her husband had to go out at night, she arranged for someone to accompany him; when he was kept in meetings late in the evening, she called on a friend to walk him home. She was at his side or thoughtful of him when danger seemed near, and she frustrated many attempts on his life. On August 28, 1525, their house was stoned at night, and the rocks sent pieces of wood flying through the house. Anna and the children were terrified, but Zwingli quieted them and seized his sword, calling out that if anyone had any business with him, they should come the next morning.

These troubles foreshadowed the sorrow that was coming to Anna. With her husband, she saw the storm gathering; it burst on October 11, 1531. On October 9, news came that the Roman Catholic army was approaching. Quickly, a little Protestant army gathered at Zurich. Zwingli went along as chaplain, and Gerold went as well. On Charity Square, just in front of the parsonage, some of the soldiers formed to march. Anna came out to say good-bye to her husband. Unable to repress her feelings, she burst into tears. The younger children, holding on to Zwingli, also cried. "The hour is come that separates us," he said to her. "Let it be so. The Lord wills."

He hugged her, and she replied, "We shall see each other again if the Lord wills. His will be done. And what will you bring back when you come?"

Zwingli's prompt reply was, "Blessing after dark night." These were his last words to her, and they comforted her for the rest of her life. She believed that the blessing would come after the dark night of earth when she saw her husband in heaven's light.

Zwingli hugged the children and left. As he rode with the soldiers and Gerold around the corner, he looked back and Anna waved a last good-bye. With the children, she hurried into the house, kneeled, and prayed the Savior's words: "Father, not my will, but Thine be done." Comforted, she got up and waited for the result of the battle.

Henry Bullinger, Zwingli's eventual successor, says that at the news of the awful defeat, a loud and horrible cry rose in Zurich. But Anna's weeping was greater, her sorrow was deeper. Anna had faced sorrows before, but this eclipsed them all. When the first news of the defeat and of her husband's death came, her friends hid the details from her, trying to soften the sorrow. Along with her husband, Gerold, a brother, and a cousin lay dead on the battlefield.[4] A son-in-law was fatally wounded. The sadness of death circled her. Then came the news that her husband's body was quartered and burned and its ashes desecrated. Was there ever sorrow like hers? Yes, there was One, of whom the prophet speaks: "Behold and see if there be any sorrow like unto my sorrow." To that Savior she went in her sorrow, and He comforted her soul.

Because of her grief, Anna has been called the Reformation's Weeping Mother. She had lost a lot, and she cried a lot. Prominent citizens and ministers visited her or wrote letters of Christian sympathy. Bucer offered to help her and the children. But the greatest comforter of all to her was young Bullinger. Just as the apostle John took Mary into his home, so Bullinger and his wife gave Anna a home and became beloved children to her. Zwingli had left his family

---

4. Bainton, *Germany and Italy*, 162.

no money; he gave all he could spare to the poor. So Bullinger took Zwingli's place as provider and cared for Anna as a son would have, saying, "You shall not want, dear mother. I will remain your friend, your teacher and adviser." He also acted as a father to Zwingli's children, supervising their education and sending young Ulrich to Basel at his own expense.

We know almost nothing of Anna's later years. Apparently, she rarely left the house after Zwingli's death, except to go to church. In her later life she was very sick, her disease continuing for years, but she bore her suffering patiently. Bullinger said of her death on December 6, 1538, "I desire no more happy end of life. She passed away softly, like a mild light, and went home to her Lord, worshipping, and commending us all to God."

Anna's oldest daughter, Regula, inherited her mother's beauty and both parents' piety. She grew up in the Bullingers' home with Rudolph Gualther, who later became her husband and succeeded Bullinger as the leader of the Zurich church.[5] During the Marian persecution in England, many refugees, including a man who later became the archbishop of Canterbury, came to Switzerland and found hospitality in Regula's home. After Regula's death her husband wrote, "What the pious Abraham lost in his beloved Sarah, and Jacob in his lovely Rachel, that have I also now to mourn. An example of purest love—of the most inviolable conjugal fidelity and domestic virtue, she knew how to drive away sadness and every tormenting care from my soul."

Beyond her support of Zwingli and all that she enabled him to do, beyond her care for the poor and sick of the parish, Anna left a living legacy in her children, who continued her pattern of building up the church through kindness to the saints. Her faithful work outlived her body.

---

5. Bullinger speaks of Regula several times in his diary, mentioning events in her life, like the birth of Regula's daughter. Heinrich Bullinger, *Heinrich Bullinger Diarium (Annales vitae) der Jahre 1504–1574* (Zurich: Theologische Buchhandlung Zürich, 1985), 61.

# 2

# Anna Adlischweiler

Like many girls in Europe, Anna Adlischweiler was donated to a convent when her family fell on hard times. But God had not planned a life of secluded chastity for this girl. Records of her birth date conflict, but it was likely in 1504. Anna's father died in battle when she was about eight years old and left her a small inheritance.[1] Her mother, a Roman Catholic, then gave Anna to the church, placing her in the Ottenbach convent at Zurich, where she became a nun. At the time, this was a common and respectable way to deal with the expense of raising a daughter. As Anna's mother was sick and convents often functioned as hospitals, she moved in with her daughter. We do not know what Anna thought of this huge shift in her life; at least convent life was predictable, governed by routine.

But while mother and daughter lived quietly in the convent, strange things happened outside of it. The Reformation had come. Zwingli's preaching had won the town, and the gospel was preached in all the churches until there was only one place that kept it out: the Ottenbach convent. The Zurich city council wanted the nuns to hear the good news and finally ordered Zwingli to go and preach to them in 1522. He obeyed with joy, preaching on the clearness and certainty of God's Word. The Word had its double effect, saving some nuns but hardening others. Bitter controversy broke out in the nunnery. The city council at last forbade the Dominican monks,

---

1. Rebecca A. Giselbrecht, "Myths and Reality about Heinrich Bullinger's Wife Anna," *Zwingliana* 38 (2011): 55.

who functioned as the nuns' spiritual guides, to enter. Zwingli and Leo Juda took over their spiritual care. The monks and some nuns protested, but in vain. The council then allowed any nuns to leave the convent if they desired, taking their clothes and any other belongings with them. Many of them took advantage of this release—some who left got married, and those who remained Roman Catholic fled to other towns. Nuns who wanted to stay were allowed to, though religious clothing was no longer permitted. Soon, except for one very old sister, Anna was the only nun left. And she could hardly be called a nun anymore; the Holy Spirit had used Zwingli's preaching to convert her. The reason she stayed was her sick mother.

As chaplain of the convent, Leo Juda took young Henry Bullinger with him one day. It was part of gaining pastoral experience, a sort of seminary field trip. They met with Anna. Bullinger quickly fell in love. Ignoring the customary practice of having a third party arrange the marriage, Bullinger proposed directly to Anna by letter.[2] It is the oldest existing love letter from a Reformer, and it stands out for its length and logic. In it, Bullinger described his physical condition and means, then wrapped up his argument by saying, "But why are many words necessary! The sum of it all is, that the greatest, surest treasure that you will find in me, is fear of God, piety, fidelity and love, which with joy I will show you, and labor, earnestness and industry, which will not be wanting in temporal things. Concerning high nobility and many thousand gulden, I can say nothing to you. But I know that what is necessary to us, will not be wanting. For Paul says, 'We brought nothing into the world, and we will take nothing out. Therefore, if we have clothing and food it is enough.'"

Although there is disagreement about when the actual—and legally binding—engagement took place, Anna accepted the proposal. Her terminally ill mother was opposed to the marriage, and Bullinger pressed his case in court, so that Anna was caught between duty to her mother and love for Bullinger. Anna postponed the

---

2. Giselbrecht, "Myths and Reality": 57.

wedding so that she could care for her mother in the convent and lived there until her mother's death.[3] Bullinger utilized the time by preparing Anna for her future position as his wife. He wrote a small book, *Concerning Female Training, and How a Daughter Should Guide Her Conduct and Life.* In 1529 Anna's mother died, and the couple married six weeks later on August 17. Bullinger recorded in his diary, "Anna and I were married in August... in the church at Birmenstorf.... I did not at all want to get married in Bremgarten in order to avoid any ostentation and a showy wedding party. A dinner reception was held in the chapel of the monastery. Our close relatives and many of the most distinguished citizens of Bremgarten" attended.[4]

The quiet wedding began a very public marriage. During the previous year, the Zurich synod had licensed Bullinger as a minister; he accepted the pastorate at Bremgarten, where his father had been pastor. The couple moved there, and Anna gave birth to two daughters, Anna and Margaret, who brought their parents much joy.[5]

But the defeat of Zurich in the same battle that killed Zwingli in 1531 made life and ministry dangerous for them, especially for Bullinger. Roman Catholics had no mercy on Protestant ministers. There is a legend about this part of Anna's life that is common in Victorian histories but does not appear in earlier accounts. It goes like this: On the night of November 20, Bullinger fled Bremgarten, along with his father and brother. They had hardly left when Roman Catholic soldiers entered the town, plundered Bullinger's house, and quartered thirty soldiers with Anna, who had stayed behind with the two little girls. Unable to feed the enemy troops and her daughters, she determined to flee too. A faithful servant, Britta, worked for the family on little pay—four gulden and a pair of shoes per year. But

---

3. Giselbrecht, "Myths and Reality": 58–59.

4. Bullinger, *Diarium*, 18. Dr. David Noe kindly translated Bullinger's entry about the wedding. The irony of a wedding dinner in a monastery is similar to the Luthers' experience of housing their large, Protestant family in the Black Cloister.

5. Bullinger, *Diarium*, 19.

she loved the Bullingers and had served the family for thirty-four years. Leaving the home in Britta's charge, Anna fled one evening with her two children, one eighteen months old, the other only six months. When she came to the gate of the town, she found it closed; the guard refused to open it. Knowing that her escape had to succeed, she tackled the guard, got the key by force, opened the gate, and fled with the babies. She arrived safely in Zurich, where her husband was staying.

Though the family did end up in Zurich, the account is exaggerated: there is no reliable record of Anna physically attacking a professional soldier. Despite that, Anna's work and efforts in other areas are equally stunning, beginning with a move to a difficult city.

The military defeat and Zwingli's death created a reaction to the Reformation in Zurich so that Leo Juda, who was serving there, was afraid to go out for fear of attack. The church at Zurich looked for a successor to Zwingli; Leo Juda convinced Bullinger to preach in the cathedral. His sermon was so able and eloquent that the people said he was Zwingli risen from the dead. Realizing that churches in Basel, Bern, and Appenzell had offered him calls, Zurich quickly voted to call him, and he accepted. This was a great honor, and it came with great responsibility not only for the preacher but also for his wife. A busy husband was only one aspect of family life; babies arrived almost yearly, until there were eleven children in the couple's home.[6] Bullinger's father and mother lived there until they died. The couple took in Zwingli's widowed wife and children, caring for them as their own family. Bullinger had the habit of inviting interns or other gifted students to live in his home: Rudolph Gualther, later his successor; two Polish boys with their tutor; and others lived with the family. He bore their living and educational costs himself.

Anna's family became large, often with more than twenty people living in her home. The wonder is that she was able to manage it

---

6. Six sons and five daughters: three of the boys died young; two became ministers, and one fought for William of Orange. All five of the daughters married pastors. Richard Rolt, *Lives of the Principle Reformers...* (London: Bakewell and Parker, 1759), 149.

all on her husband's small salary. Great economy was necessary to feed and clothe so many. We have hints of her difficulty in a letter that Bullinger wrote in December 1553 to his oldest son, who was at Strasbourg: "Your mother makes big eyes when you already speak of needing another pair of shoes for the winter. It is hardly fifteen weeks since you left us, when you took three pairs with you, the red, the gray and black. At this rate you will need six pairs a year. I have more than enough with two.... Do not let your shoes go to pieces, but get them mended in time." On his small salary, Bullinger could not have provided for everyone in his home if Anna had not been frugal. And she could not have done all she did without the help of her mother-in-law and Britta, who had also made it safely to Zurich and was still much loved. Writing to his son Henry in 1556, Bullinger commented, "Your five sisters greet you, and especially Britta, who sends to you a present of three groschen." Britta might be the Reformation's model servant. Little did she think that her faithfulness would be spoken of 450 years after her ministry in Bullinger's home.

A large, diverse family was not the only recipient of Anna's care. Her house was a home to the homeless, as Protestant refugees from all over Europe came to stay. Zurich was an asylum to the persecuted Reformed believers of other countries, and Bullinger was a good friend to the refugees. First, in 1542, came the Italian Reformed: Peter Martyr, Bernard Ochino, and Celio Curione. Curione wrote a letter of thanks, in which he called Bullinger a bishop according to the apostle Paul's description, and said, "Your friendliness and your Christian care for us during our stay with you obliges me to give you my inmost thanks. Greet for us very heartily your wife, who showed herself so full of kindly service and love." Then came the refugees from Locarno, on the southern border of Switzerland; on March 3, 1556, they fled over the snow-covered Alps. On May 12, 116 of them arrived at Zurich. Bullinger and Anna set the example of hospitality for the city. When persecution broke out in England in 1550 under Mary I, Bullinger and the Zurich church gladly received the refugees. Even before that, as early as 1536, Archbishop Cranmer had sent three young men to be educated at Zurich, two of whom Bullinger took into his own house. One of them would later repeatedly express his thankfulness to Bullinger and to Anna, who had become a mother to him.

Because of the persecution in England, Bullinger's table was often filled with refugees, and Anna sometimes worried about what to do with them or how to feed and clothe them all. Somehow, she managed; the Lord always provided. In 1546, Bishop Hooper fled to Zurich with his family; they lived in the Bullinger home, and their daughter was baptized there. The city founded a school to educate English students as ministers, five of whom later became Anglican bishops; they all expressed thankfulness to Bullinger and Anna for their kind hospitality. The couple's care for the English Protestants was so well known that Queen Elizabeth later sent an ornamental goblet to them to express her thanks. But refugees continued coming. When the wars in Germany went against the Protestants, some of them found refuge at Zurich. One of them later sent a letter thanking Bullinger for his hospitality and Anna for the comfort she gave his wife. So Anna ministered to many refugee believers.

But Anna's visitors were not limited to those fleeing persecution. Her husband's talents and position brought prominent foreign guests: Calvin and Farel from Geneva; Bucer and Capito from Strasbourg; Portalis, the king of Navarre's ambassador; noble families of Wurtemburg and Schaumburg. The Bullinger home welcomed all of them. Besides the foreign visitors who came and found shelter, Anna also took in the poor of Zurich and cared for them. A continual stream of gifts flowed through Anna's hands to the city's poor. She provided the needy sick with food, drink, clothing, and money—everything necessary—and was joined by other local pastors' wives in these labors of love. It is no wonder that in Zurich people called her mother. And in other countries, English, Italians, Dutch, and Germans called her the "Zurich mother."

Anna proved faithful to the end. In 1564 her husband contracted the plague, and everyone thought he would die. Anna nursed him so that he recovered, but at the cost of her own life. As he strengthened, she sickened and died. All Zurich mourned.[7] People encouraged Bullinger to remarry after Anna's death, but he refused, because he loved Anna, who was "still living in his heart."[8]

Her life remains a beautiful example of faithful love and self-sacrifice for all God's people. Though it must have seemed like drudgery to her at times, Anna's work brought comfort to hundreds each year, allowed young men to prepare for future ministry, and enabled her husband to further the gospel cause in the place where God had put this faithful couple. One of her husband's best-known books, *Christian Matrimony*, reflects the happy marriage pattern that Anna and her husband seemed to have had; they spread this pattern throughout Europe.[9] Anna's example as helpmeet became the Protestant standard for many decades.

---

7. Three of Anna's adult daughters also died in the same epidemic in 1564 and 1565. Rolt, *Lives of Reformers*, 149.

8. As quoted in Rolt, *Lives of Reformers*, 149.

9. Heinrich Bullinger, *The Christen State of Matrimonye*, trans. Miles Coverdale, facsimile of the 1541 ed. (Amsterdam: Theatrum Orbis Terrarum, Ltd, 1974). For centuries, this was the best seller on marriage and home life. William Gouge based his best-selling *Domestical Duties* on Bullinger's work.

# 3
## Katharina Schütz

Zwingli praised Matthew Zell's wife, Katharina: "She combines the graces of both Mary and Martha." Intense and capable, Katharina acted as a mother to many Protestant refugees and became the early Reformation's leading female author. Sometimes called the Mother Reformer, she spent herself in gospel service.

Katharina Schütz (c. 1497–1562) was born in Strasbourg. She came from a comfortably established artisan family that gave the children—daughters included—a good education. At a young age she developed religious zeal and even made vows of chastity. This was a sign of deep Roman Catholic piety, but despite her devotion, Katharina struggled with assurance of salvation, feeling that her attendance at Mass, charitable deeds, and confessions were never enough to earn God's favor. But during her late teens, changes took place in Strasbourg. New doctrines and books were introduced, and around 1518 Matthew Zell arrived to be the preacher at the great cathedral. He soon began preaching the gospel—the same theology that was getting Luther into so much trouble at the time.

This made waves. The Roman Catholic archbishop, in authority over the cathedral, did not let Zell into the pulpit, a towerlike structure with its own stairs and a door. As this was literally locked, Zell's friends made a wooden pulpit that they carried into the church whenever Zell was about to preach; from this temporary spot, he spoke to crowds that filled the vast building. Increasingly, his sermons attacked the errors of Roman Catholicism, especially Marian adoration, and replaced error with scriptural truth. Combined with

Protestant publications coming from Strasbourg's presses, the biblical truth of Zell's sermons largely turned the city to Protestantism.[1] In the congregation was Zell's future wife, Katharina, who accepted biblical doctrine with typical earnestness. Her search for spiritual security was gone; assurance of salvation came with an understanding of Christ's completed work and the Spirit's sanctifying work.

Pastor and parishioner were married December 3, 1525.[2] The men of Strasbourg filled the cathedral to show their approval of their priest's marriage. Martin Bucer, who later took up Zell's role of Strasbourg Reformer, performed the ceremony. When it was over, the people celebrated the Lord's Supper in the Reformed manner. Katharina proved to be a pious, busy, discreet wife, fully supportive of her husband, who was twenty years older than she.[3] Katharina often thanked God for the unity between them and said that she and Zell were "of one mind and one soul." She wrote, "What bound us together was not silver and gold. Both of us possessed a higher thing, 'Christ was the mark before our eyes.'" It was one of the first Protestant marriages, and it was a bold step for both husband and wife; priests who married broke canon law, defied Rome, and sometimes lost their position and their income.[4] But in the Zells' case, it was a step that the Lord blessed. The energy that Katharina had formerly put into religious exercises to save her soul she now poured into her marriage and the Reformation.

As she was well educated, Katharina's growing understanding of the Bible gave her a deep knowledge of religion. Blessed with courage and eloquence, she understood how to defend her views in person and by pen. Her great aim was to spread the gospel. Sometimes it seemed as if she outdid her husband in this, so that he seemed to be in the background; with a shrug, Bucer said that Zell

1. Alise Anne McKee, *Katharina Schütz Zell* (Leiden: Brill, 1999), 1:34–35.

2. McKee, *Katharina Schütz Zell*, 1:40.

3. Bainton, *Germany and Italy*, 56.

4. McKee, *Katharina Schütz Zell*, 1:47.

was ruled by his wife, who was "a trifle imperious."[5] But Bucer also bore witness that she was "as God-fearing and courageous as a hero," and because Zell began reforming before his marriage, we cannot put him in the shadow of a controlling wife. Katharina herself said that she only wanted to be her husband's helpmeet—a "little piece of the rib of the sainted Matthew Zell."

One of her best-known works is a defense of clerical marriage, showing from Scripture why priests and pastors have the right to marry and why celibacy is not morally superior to marriage. This was not only to refute false accusations against her husband but also to help people rethink the issue so that priests would see biblical reasons to marry and parishioners would allow their daughters to wed ordained men. Katharina identified the people slandering her husband, calling them each names—"wolf," "poison spewer," "fool"—for teaching against clerical marriage. Throwing their arguments back at them, Katharina stated that the Roman Catholic position against clerical marriage was not based on Scripture but on the pope's system of taxing the rampant prostitution among the clergy.[6] She closed with a quote from Isaiah 57:3–4:

> But come here,
> You sons of the sorceress,
> You offspring of the adulterer and the harlot!
> Whom do you ridicule?
> Against whom do you make a wide mouth
> And stick out the tongue?
> Are you not children of transgression,
> Offspring of falsehood?

Katharina's behavior counters the stereotype of a helpmeet being spineless and needy. Her direct and frank rebuttal made her known

---

5. As quoted in Bainton, *Germany and Italy*, 63.

6. Katharina Schütz Zell, *Church Mother: The Writings of a Protestant Reformer in Sixteenth-Century Germany*, trans. Elsie McKee (Chicago: University of Chicago Press, 2006), 72–73.

throughout Europe. Katharina's private correspondence became pro-
lific, and she excelled at it. Soon after her marriage she began writing
Luther; she also exchanged letters with Zwingli.

She was busy in her community as well, caring for the sick,
needy, and Protestant refugees who fled to Strasbourg because of persecution: "I have already in the beginning of my marriage received
many excellent and learned people in their flight, and comforted
them as God has said: 'Support and strengthen the weak knees.'"
When fifteen Protestant men had to flee from Baden for conscience's
sake, the Zells took in an old doctor. Later, he was in a Roman
Catholic prison for four years and said that his memories of Katharina's kindness comforted him. In 1524, 150 men were driven out
of Kentzingen in one night and fled to Strasbourg. Zell welcomed
eighty of them into his house; Katharina kindly cared for them, feed-
ing fifty or sixty for four weeks. She also wrote a letter to their wives,
encouraging them to stand firm in their faith. More than pity, the
letter offered the women reason to be joyful and bold in their faith;
their suffering was evidence of their election.[7] It also put a woman's
role of staying at home with children in the category of active service
to Christ, not a default or passive position.[8] "Would that God," she
wrote, "would regard me with such grace and favor, and favor me
with such great honor so that I should have gifts unlike yet also like
yours, to suffer such things with His dearest Christ with you."[9]

At that time, the Reformed faith required fortitude from every
adherent. During the Peasants' War, which broke out in 1525, Katharina accompanied her husband and other ministers in visiting the
camps to plead with people to stop the violence; their advice went
unheeded, and three thousand more refugees poured into Strasbourg, which had a population of only about twenty-five thousand.[10]

7. McKee, *Katharina Schütz Zell*, 2:2; Zell, *Church Mother*, 50, 53.

8. Zell, *Church Mother*, 43.

9. Zell, "Letter to the Suffering Women of the Community of Kentzingen," in
*Church Mother*, 52–53.

10. Bainton, *Germany and Italy*, 63.

Katharina was continually busy caring for such refugees. When she could not help, she recruited others. This aspect of her work was not only a blessing to many refugees but it also strengthened her marriage, as Zell delighted in her service, which was a joint endeavor. At their wedding Zell had commissioned her to be a "mother to the poor and refugees"—she only did what both of them thought God wanted her to.[11]

Katharina was also a regular visitor to the local prison; the inmates' religious views varied, but she spoke with many who spent time there. Her compassion for the men led her to make time for these visits despite her demanding schedule that could easily have crowded them out.[12]

Many great Reformers fled to Katharina's home during persecution. When Bucer fled from Weissenburg, he found a refuge and home in Mrs. Zell's house. When Calvin fled France, all his money stolen on the way, Katharina gave him a warm welcome at her fireside. In 1529, when the debate between Luther and Zwingli at Marburg brought so many Reformers to Strasbourg, Katharina exerted herself to host these pastors. She said, "I have been for fourteen days maid and cook while the dear men Oecolampadius and Zwingli were here."

Family also took up Katharina's time. Her relatives were locals: parents, sisters, their husbands, nieces, and nephews were welcome at the Zell home. After Katharina's mother died, her father moved into a house close to the Zells, where he lived with his four unmarried children. Their care was probably a regular part of Katharina's routine. And Katharina gave birth to her own baby as well, likely in 1526.[13] Both parents were thrilled. Katharina was still busy with charity work and hospitality; motherhood did not entirely eclipse her other biblical callings. But in February 1527, the baby died. Biographer

---

11. McKee, *Katharina Schütz Zell*, 1:50.

12. Bainton, *Germany and Italy*, 65.

13. McKee, *Katharina Schütz Zell*, 1:70.The birth date is an estimate based on the baptismal register.

Alise McKee writes, "Matthew seemed to cope better, but Katharina especially struggled."[14] Sometime around a period of serious illness in 1531, Katharina gave birth to a second baby. It is unclear how long this child lived, but by 1533 it too had died.[15] In addition to a mother's grief, Katharina the theologian worried that the deaths were some sort of chastisement from God.[16] Friends assured her they were not, but her grief was great, and she struggled to understand.

Though the double loss was a deep valley for Katharina, it does not seem to have slowed her service to others or her care for the church. Her husband was not lacking in courage for the truth, as his boldness in preaching showed. Still, he was inclined to quietness in the controversies that raged among the Protestants. But Katharina was not afraid of controversy, writing publicly for truth and peace wherever she felt it was needed. She wrote to Luther, asking him to treat the Swiss with a little more mildness in the controversy about the Lord's Supper, and received a more polite reply than Luther usually wrote. After the Wittenberg Concord of 1536 brought peace between Luther and the Swiss, the Zells took a journey to Wittenberg, which Katharina enjoyed very much.

While she was a staunch advocate for the truth, she was also sympathetic toward the Anabaptists and even the Schwenkfelder sect.[17] When Schwenkfeld came to Strasbourg as a refugee in 1528, Katharina received him with kindness. Bucer, dubious again, said that Schwenkfeld's manners and artificially pious attitude allowed him greater access to the Zells than he otherwise would have had.[18]

---

14. McKee, *Katharina Schütz Zell*, 1:77.

15. McKee, *Katharina Schütz Zell*, 2:306.

16. McKee, *Katharina Schütz Zell*, 1:84.

17. Initially a Lutheran, Schwenkfeld became increasingly sectarian, rejecting infant baptism and denominations and promoting pacifism and other doctrines similar to the Anabaptists. Schwenkfeld eventually wandered into heresy, teaching biblically indefensible theories about Christ's human and divine natures. Finding themselves at theological odds with most of Europe, many of his followers immigrated to Pennsylvania.

18. Bainton, *Germany and Italy*, 66.

Whatever the cause, Katharina defended Schwenkfeld publicly and corresponded with him.

During a time of plague in 1641, Katharina nursed many people in Strasbourg—including her husband—back to health.[19] Once more, she saw a clear calling to serve, and her fearless obedience shone. It was not the last time that care for the sick would increase her fame in the city and beyond.

Her great labors aged her. But she was still active when the Lord called her husband away by death on January 9, 1548. On the last night of his life, he told Katharina to give his last message to his assistant pastors, asking them "to leave the Anabaptists and Schwenkfelders in peace, and to preach Christ rather than persecute them." The day of Zell's funeral was the same day that the citizens renewed their oath to the city and elected their magistrates; thousands of the men in town followed Zell's coffin to its grave. After Bucer had preached the funeral sermon and many people had gone home, Katharina spoke to close friends about her husband's work and last words of love. This address was later published. Out of respect for Zell, the city magistrates allowed Katharina to stay in the cathedral parsonage, which kept her from poverty.

Despite her own failing health, Katharina continued her care for the sick. In 1558 one of the city magistrates contracted leprosy. His own family was denied visitation, but Katharina somehow gained permission to see him, regularly encouraging him in his affliction.[20] There was also a nephew with syphilis who was sent to a hospital for people with the disease. Feeling a family burden for him, Katharina lived with him in the hospital for a time, giving him the quality care that the staff did not.

In the year before Matthew Zell's death, Charles V had tried to introduce the Augsburg Interim, which forced people to return to Roman Catholic practice. Katharina wrote publicly against

---

19. McKee, *Katharina Schütz Zell*, 1:107.

20. Bainton, *Germany and Italy*, 68.

it, imploring Strasbourg to give up the pope and remain true to Christ. But after Zell's death and Bucer's departure for England, Strasbourg changed. Lutheranism was introduced to the city, and Katharina became involved in her most public and painful controversy. When her husband was alive, a student, Rabus, lived in their home as an intern. He became Zell's successor and the city's most popular preacher. Although trained by the Zells, he began attacking Reformed views and customs, urging high Lutheranism. Katharina's tolerance did not extend to one abusing her husband's pulpit and theology, so she wrote against Rabus. Her writings against him are the most notable of her works, as their defense of truth and their public, controversial nature placed Katharina in the role of Reformer. In 1557, Rabus answered her; the letters move from theological-political issues to personal attacks on Katharina, whom he called "disturber of the peace of the church." She replied in a letter to the whole citizenship of Strasbourg. Her language was severe and her defense eloquent: "Do you call this disturbing the peace that instead of spending my time in frivolous amusements I have visited the plague infested and carried out the dead? I have visited those in prison and under sentence of death. Often for three days and nights I have neither eaten or slept. I have never mounted the pulpit, but I have done more than any minister in visiting those in ministry. Is this disturbing the peace of the church?" And later: "You young fellows tread on the graves of the first fathers of this church in Strasbourg and punish all who disagree with you, but faith cannot be forced."[21] It was a time that caused her sorrow.

By 1558, Katharina's study of the Scriptures, partly flowing out of her grief at Matthew's death, theological divisions, and a friend's suffering, was published.[22] A commentary on Psalms 51 and 130 and the Lord's Prayer, it is more meditative than her other writings,

---

21. Katharina Schütz Zell to Rabus, in Bainton, *Germany and Italy*, 72, 73.
22. McKee, *Katharina Schütz Zell*, 2:305–9.

showing an author spiritually developed by the means of grace and grief. It was her last published work.

She continued to be the refuge of persecuted Protestants from all denominations. Before Bucer left for England, he gave her two gold pieces to facilitate her care for refugees. She divided one of them between a persecuted minister with five children and a pastor's widow who had seen her husband beheaded. The other piece she returned to Bucer, thinking he would need it in England. So she continued her labors of love till she died. The date of her death is unknown. She was living still on March 3, 1562; a letter she wrote that day survives, saying that she could not write much because she was "often half dead with her long sickness, and could not hold the pen." Even then, at an old sixty-four, she was trying to instruct and encourage others in the faith through correspondence. Certainly by the end of that year, she was in glory.

She must have anticipated death for a while before it came; a few years earlier she had written her thoughts about it to a friend:

> I see before my eyes and welcome the time of my release; I rejoice in it, and know that to die here will be my gain, that I lay aside the mortal and perishable and put on the everlasting immortal and imperishable. I am now sixty years old, and I have walked before God in fear of Him and despising the world for fifty years, so that I can say with the holy Ambrose: "I have lived so that I am not ashamed to continue to live among the faithful, but I do not fear to die, for I am certain that in Christ I will live again and that in Him I have a gracious God forever."[23]

That was the testimony of one of the foremost women of the Reformation church, the childless Mother Reformer whose abilities equaled her husband's. While she excelled in managing her home and hosting refugees, she also defended her theological position in print.

---

23. Katharina Schütz Zell to Armbruster, July 1558, in McKee, *Katharina Schütz Zell,* 1:229.

She was a female theologian in the best sense. Historians today call her a lay Reformer. But she only did what every Christian should: she used her gifts for gospel change in her own sphere in whatever ways possible.

# 4

## *Margarethe Blaurer*

Among Reformation women, there are sisters of Reformers as well as wives. Margarethe Blaurer (c. 1494–1541) was the sister of Ambrose Blaurer, the Reformer of Konstanz and Württemberg. Though we have less information about her than most of the other women, she provides an example of service in singleness.[1]

In 1415, Huss had been burned at the stake in Konstanz, predicting that the Reformation would rise from his ashes. In 1527, the city threw off Roman Catholicism. More than twenty ministers preached the gospel in churches that had removed statues and icons, and Roman Catholic priests and bishops fled the city. In this Reformed place, the Blaurer family became prominent. Ambrose had been a monk but left the monastery because he was disgusted with the religious community's sins. His brother Thomas became burgomaster, and Margarethe became the Swiss Reformation's helpmeet.

During the Reformation, Konstanz struggled through many trials: drought, plague, and earthquake came one after the other. During all of these, Margarethe was a great help to Ambrose. Like so many other Protestant women, she was well educated, despite her common birth. James Good says that Erasmus and Bullinger honored her as a poetess, but it seems as though her Latin was lacking;

---

1. James Good spelled Margarethe's last name Blaarer; Bucer spelled it Blaurer in his correspondence. See, for example, *Martin Bucer Briefwechsel, Band III (1527–1529)* (Leiden: Brill, 1995), 107. Blarer is a more common modern spelling, though the family seems to have preferred Blaurer.

surviving letters to her are in her own tongue. She corresponded with many Reformation scholars. On his way home from a conference in 1528, Bucer returned to Germany by way of Konstanz. There, he met Margarethe and afterward wrote several letters to her.[2] He addressed her as "sister" and even "mother," though he was only three years older, using this title for her out of respect. Bucer was a guest more than once in the Blaurer home. He once ate there while Margarethe was away; Ambrose later wrote to Bucer that Margarethe was disappointed that she was not able to host him herself and asked him to come again when she would be able to serve him.[3]

The relationship between Margarethe and Bucer is fairly typical of the friendships that male Reformers had with female correspondents. Bucer's primary relationship was with Margarethe's brother, and often when Bucer wrote to Ambrose, he would include greetings to Margarethe in the conclusion of his letter. But because of her involvement in reform work, Bucer sometimes encouraged and advised her directly. They knew each other well enough for Bucer to tease Margarethe to end her singleness with a good marriage; even back then, pastors were tempted to match up godly young people. He also asked for Margarethe's help in arranging a match between a young man he thought highly of and a young woman whom Margarethe knew.[4]

Theology was also a topic of discussion. The Anabaptists were making waves in the Protestant community, and Margarethe had friends among them. Bucer explained the danger of the group's theological trajectory, calling the teaching heresy. Whether Margarethe

---

2. Good claims that seventy-nine are in a Zurich archive, but he has no references, so these letters are difficult to locate. Good, *Famous Women of the Reformed Church*, 56. Brill's multivolume publication of Bucer's letters contains several to Margarethe, but not nearly the number that Good claims. There are many more letters to Ambrose in Bucer's correspondence. *Martin Bucer Briefwechsel, Band III.*

3. Ambrose Blauer to Martin Bucer, February 13, 1531, in *Martin Bucer Briefwechsel/ Correspondence Band V (September 1530–Mai 1531)* (Leiden: Brill, 2004), 271.

4. *Martin Bucer Briefwechsel, Band VI (Mai–October 1531)* (Leiden: Brill, 2006), 25.

was considering their views as scriptural or whether Bucer feared she might is unclear. He did send her "our confession"—a scriptural explanation of the errors she saw.[5] So, like many of her Protestant peers, Margarethe also read theological works in the spare time she carved out.

In their discussions of mutual friends, relationships, and larger issues of reform, it is clear that the Reformer and the Reformer's sister were friends in a biblical way, encouraging each other as they did the work of reform and offering practical help—two parts of a network trying to facilitate the advance of the gospel.

Though she was honored by prominent Reformers, Margarethe remained modest and hardworking. Reflecting on Margarethe, whose name means "pearl," Good says, "She had not only found the pearl of great price, but was a pearl herself through the splendor of her piety and her example of good works." Her faith was a blessing to the city; she was untiring in doing good. She taught many poor children to read and visited widows and orphans to comfort them. While Ambrose reformed the church from his pulpit and Thomas led the city from his council room, her work was a labor of love that reached everyone in town. She founded and organized the first Protestant women's society to care for the sick, a necessary alternative in a time when female community was limited to convents. When plague broke out in 1541, she labored hard among the sick, risking her own life. Her brother Ambrose wrote to Bullinger on November 5, 1541, that the plague was sweeping the town, taking many children as well as adults. Near the end of the letter, he described his sister as "arch deaconess of our church," putting her life in danger by visiting homes with the plague every day. During this time, Margarethe also took in a young girl who now needed more care than Margarethe had given her for years. Ambrose understood the danger in which this placed his beloved sister. He closed the letter by asking Bullinger

---

5. Martin Bucer to Margarethe Blaurer, August 31, 1531, in *Martin Bucer Briefwechsel/Correspondence Band VI*, 93.

to pray that the Lord would not take away Margarethe, "who is our only comfort."[6]

The Lord saw fit to refuse this request; Margarethe died November 15, 1541. She was forty-seven. On November 30 Ambrose wrote to Bullinger that he and the church had lost a most faithful deaconess and that there was "great mourning everywhere."[7] Bullinger answered, sharing the brother's grief that his sister had been "snatched" away and pointing him to consolation in the Lord.[8] Other men joined Bullinger in comforting Ambrose, who felt the loss deeply.[9] He wrote a hymn full of Christian hope upon Margarethe's death. He was one of the earliest hymn writers among the Reformed, and he used his gifts to comfort himself and the churches in the city.

It was good that Margarethe died when she did. In God's mercy she did not live a few years longer to see the Reformed driven out of Konstanz and forced to flee to Switzerland. When that storm burst on the city, Margarethe was safe with her Lord in heaven. Her brother has been called the Apostle of Württemberg; Margarethe might well be called the Angel of Mercy of Konstanz.

---

6. Ambrose Blaurer to Heinrich Bullinger, November 5, 1541, in Ambrose Blarer and Thomas Blarer, *Briefwechsel der Bruder Ambrosius und Thomas Blaurer, 1509–1548, Band III* (Stuttgart: Freiburg i. Br., 1910), 90–91.

7. Ambrose Blaurer to Heinrich Bullinger, November 30, 1541, in Blarer and Blarer, *Briefwechsel der Bruder Ambrosius und Thomas Blaurer*, 93. Ambrose wrote about his grief more than once to Bullinger, with whom he seems to have been close.

8. Heinrich Bullinger to Ambrose Blaurer, December 10, 1541, in Blarer and Blarer, *Briefwechsel der Bruder Ambrosius und Thomas Blaurer*, 94.

9. Bonifacius Wolfhart, Conrad Hubert, Rudolf Gualther, in Blarer and Blarer, *Briefwechsel der Bruder Ambrosius und Thomas Blaurer*, 98–111.

# 5
## Marguerite de Navarre

The first princess to become Reformed was Marguerite de Navarre.[1] Even at the beginning of the Reformation, Bible doctrine reached thrones. French Reformed Christians owed Marguerite much: if it had not been for her influence and protection, they would have been crushed before the French church could form. Her influence and work opened the way for her descendants to further the Reformation in France.

She was born April 2, 1492, at Angouleme.[2] Her brother Francois was in line for the French throne. Marguerite shared the excellent education he received. It was unusual for girls to be educated alongside boys, even if they were siblings, and Marguerite benefited from this training: fluent in French, Spanish, English, Hebrew, Latin, with some Italian and German, she understood philosophy, history, literature, and theology.[3] At age seventeen, in 1509, she married Charles, Duke of Alençon. Not much older than Marguerite, Charles was not an evil man, but he was his wife's inferior in looks, abilities, and piety. The marriage was merely politically convenient and produced no children during its sixteen years. It seems that during this time,

---

1. Navarre, now an autonomous Spanish region bordering France, was a small kingdom in the western Pyrenees Mountains.

2. She is sometimes called Marguerite d'Anjouleme to distinguish her from Margaret of Navarre (c. 1135–1183) and Margaret Valois, queen of Navarre (1553–1615), who was also a published authoress.

3. Carol Thysell, *The Pleasure of Discernment: Marguerite de Navarre as Theologian* (Oxford: Oxford University Press, 2000), 6.

evangelical preaching and discussions with others brought Marguerite to saving faith.[4]

Francois I, king of France, was Marguerite's only brother; they were unusually close siblings.[5] Francois's wife, Queen Claude, was chronically ill, so Marguerite often functioned as queen for her brother and was present at court, hosting and directing things that her sister-in-law could not. When Claude died, Marguerite raised two of Francois's daughters as her own. Someone once complained to him that Marguerite was inclining to Protestantism, and he replied, "If what you say is true, I love her too well to allow her to be troubled on that account." He often told her enemies, "My sister Marguerite is the only woman I ever knew who had every virtue and every grace without any admixture of vice." So in the Roman Catholic court, Marguerite was able to speak of Christ, and, through her influence, many of the nobility became Reformed. Using her position to spread and protect Protestantism, she hoped that Francois would become Europe's political defender of Protestantism.[6]

But early in his rule, Francois began to see Protestantism as dangerous; individuals who pushed for reform were targeted. When Marguerite was once away from Paris, a friend of hers from the university was arrested, dragged through the streets of the city followed by a mob, and put in prison. His cell was small, dark, and partly

---

4. Bishop Briconnet, inclined to an evangelical mysticism, had great influence on Marguerite's theology, though her beliefs were later tempered by Scripture reading and by the influence of Reformed chaplains. Her own writing hints that reading the book of Jeremiah may have been instrumental in her conversion. Marguerite de Navarre, "Mirror of the Sinful Soul," in *Selected Writings*, ed. and trans. Rouben Cholakian and Mary Skemp (Chicago: University of Chicago Press, 2008), 113.

5. This is the same Francois to whom Calvin dedicated his *Institutes of the Christian Religion*.

6. In addition to interceding for condemned Protestants, Marguerite also wanted convents to reform. This not only points to her evangelical interest in correcting the problems of Roman Catholicism but also her support of the existence of these institutions, which she believed could be useful. Susan Broomhall, *Women and Religion in Sixteenth-Century France* (New York: Palgrave MacMillan, 2006), 21, 28, 56–57, 79.

filled with water. There was no space where he could sit down, only a spot where he could crouch with his back against the damp stone wall. Here he was kept without light and fresh air and was given little food for days. But suddenly the cell door opened, and he found himself free. He knew Marguerite had done this. When he staggered through the Paris streets, not even his old friends would speak to him or help; persecution had made them afraid. He determined to go to the palace. Standing like a beggar at the gate, he wrote a note to Marguerite, stating his condition. She immediately ordered him into her presence. When he reached her drawing room, she, looking every bit the French princess, was surrounded by ambassadors and servants. She rose to meet him, introduced him to everyone, and then sent him to a suite where everything was done for his comfort. It seems that as soon as she had returned to the city and heard of her friend's imprisonment, she had begged her brother with tears for his release. Francois granted it, finding it difficult to refuse her.

Clement Marot, a Protestant poet and Marguerite's valet, was then arrested. He spent his time in prison writing poems, and because of Marguerite's influence, he was soon free too. It would have been a great loss to the French Reformed church if she had not pushed for his release; he authored the French translation of the Psalms, which that church sang for centuries.

Louis de Berquin, one of the most learned of the French nobles, was arrested in 1523 for his evangelical ideas but was released through Marguerite's influence. Two years later, he was again arrested and interrogated. When the Roman Catholics urged him to observe some Roman Catholic rite to save his life, he replied, "I will not yield a single point." He expected to be burned at the stake, but Marguerite gained liberty for him in 1526. But in 1529, Berquin was arrested and imprisoned a third time for his faith. Marguerite again used all her efforts to have him released, but in vain. Francois could be pushed only so far on an issue that was public. To Marguerite's great sorrow, Berquin was martyred on April 22, 1529.

Grieved but still seeking to bring gospel truth to her nation, Marguerite tried to bring back French Reformers who, like the evangelical priest Jacques Lefevre, had fled from France to safety in other countries. She petitioned her brother, who allowed them to return for a time; Melanchthon was also permitted to visit France. Marguerite showed herself unafraid of persecution and association with the persecuted.

Marguerite also had diplomatic ability, which Francois admired. In February 1525, Charles V captured Francois in battle and took him back to Spain as a prisoner. Marguerite traveled there, caring for her brother until his release, which she negotiated.[7] Her time in court had given her an education in international relations as well as in manners.

The same battle that left Francois a prisoner left Marguerite a widow: the duke had been killed in action. Later that year, she married the king of Navarre, Henri d'Albret. The wedding was splendid; the marriage was not. Leaving Paris for her new capital, Nerac, she left Francois to rule alone in a way that he previously had not. Marguerite and Henri had only two children, one of whom died as a baby.

In her writings, which speak in clear and moving terms of the soul's espousal to Christ, Marguerite's mind went upward to a better marriage:

> Lord, when shall come that festal day
> So ardently desired
> That I shall by love upraised
> And seated at thy side,
> The rapture of this nuptial joy
> Denudes me quite.[8]

Her husband's kingdom was untouched by Reformation doctrines. Marguerite began spreading them by her example and influence. Roman Catholic Henri was not pleased with this, and

---

7. Thysell, *Pleasure of Discernment*, 7.

8. In Roland H. Bainton, *Women of the Reformation in France and England* (Minneapolis: Fortress, 2007), 37. See also de Navarre, "Mirror of the Sinful Soul," in *Selected Writings*, 87–89, 93, 103, 107, 111.

eventually things came to a head. Marguerite usually had private evangelical services in her apartments, with Lefevre or Roussel preaching. One day they celebrated the Lord's Supper. In the palace, there was an underground hall beneath the terrace called the Mint. Here, Marguerite's servants quietly placed a table, covered it with a white cloth, and laid out bread and wine. Joined by other Protestants in the castle, Marguerite took part in the Supper.

Though the Communion service was held secretly, news of it got to the king, who had been out hunting and was greatly annoyed by the "fastings in the cellar." He asked where Marguerite was. Told that she was in her apartments listening to a preacher, he went there. The minister and others were warned and escaped. Marguerite was alone with her servants to receive him. Flushed with anger over her theological positions and lack of submission, Henri struck her in the face, saying, "Madame, you know too much." This was too great an insult to be passed over, and Marguerite reported it to her brother. The thought of anyone hitting his sister was too much for Francois, who immediately set out for Navarre, threatening war. The news of his coming filled Henri with fear. He begged his wife to forgive him—he was so penitent that he promised to allow Reformed worship and read about Reformed doctrine himself. War was avoided, and Henri kept his bargain. Marguerite grew in her faith:

> If they tell you that in some other place,
> One can find solace
> And true salvation, other than in one God,
> They mean to destroy your soul;
> Take a firm stand.[9]

But love for a sister did not color Francois's strengthening religious position. Time at the committed Roman Catholic court in Madrid had a lasting effect; on his return, he banned Protestant books and was careful not to invite his sister's Protestant friends to court. "She

---

9. Marguerite de Navarre, "Song," in *Selected Writings*, 289.

wanted to reform the church because God willed it," writes Bainton. "Franc[o]is wanted to reform the church because he controlled it."[10] Surprised and grieved, Marguerite wrote more poetry:

> O You my Priest, my Advocate, my King,
> On whom depends my life, my everything;
> O Lord, who first did drain the bitter cup of woe,
> And knows its poison (if man e'er did know),
> These thorns how sharp, these wounds how deep—
> Saviour, Friend, King, oh, plead my cause, I pray;
> Speak, help, and save me, lest I fall away.

Marguerite's daughter, Jeanne, was born in France in 1528. Francois took the child away in 1530 to raise her as a French princess—a Roman Catholic—away from her mother's evangelistic ideas. So her only living child was taken away because she was Protestant.[11] Marguerite paid a high price for her public faith—perhaps the highest price a mother can pay. Still, she did not allow this grief to end her service to the Reformed church.

In 1533 she became Protestantism's first published female poet with the release of a volume of religious poems titled *The Mirror of the Sinful Soul*—a commentary on the words "Create in me a clean heart, O Lord."[12] In the poem, she dwells on Christ's great sacrifice for sin and the soul's union to Christ. Still shedding Roman

---

10. Bainton, *France and England*, 14.

11. It became increasingly common, especially among Protestant families of position and influence, for their children to be taken from them and raised as Roman Catholics. The Huguenot pastor Jean Claude later wrote that this was one of the reasons for the mass exodus of the French Reformed to the Low Countries: "The horror of seeing their consciences forced, their children abducted, & of having to live henceforth in a land where there will be neither justice nor compassion for them, obliged everyone to think of an escape." As quoted in David van der Linden, *Experiencing Exile: Huguenot Refugees in the Dutch Republic, 1680–1700* (Farnham, U.K.: Ashgate, 2015), 15.

12. De Navarre, *Selected Writings*, 73.

Catholicism, she shows an unbiblical admiration for Mary, but a clear understanding that salvation is through Christ alone:

> And what is more, I see that none other than
> Jesus Christ is my plaintiff....
> He has made himself
> Our advocate before God, offering up virtues of such worth
> That my debt is more than paid....
> Sweet Jesus...you have been placed here
> to speak on my behalf and to forgive
> Where you could easily have accused.[13]

The mysticism in her early writings is typical of a female author in the Roman Catholic Church, but the reverence for God's Word in them is not.

Roman Catholics were so angry with the work that some students wrote and performed an allegorical play that ridiculed Marguerite. The faculty of theology at Sorbonne condemned the volume as evangelistic—even "Lutheran."[14] This was a dangerous accusation. Undeterred, Marguerite continued writing. Though her brother made the faculty retract their censure, this open association with Protestantism put a divide between brother and sister that slowly widened.

The next year, in the fall, satirical posters mocking the Roman Catholic Mass appeared all over Paris, including at the palace. The anonymous attack went too far; Francois hardened himself against the Huguenot church and ordered the execution of all "heretics."[15] When Marguerite found she could no longer use her influence to advance Protestantism, she used her position to protect it. During the persecutions, whenever Marguerite was in Paris, her brother would not allow any Protestants to be martyred out of respect for his

---

13. De Navarre, "Mirror of the Sinful Soul," in *Selected Writings*, 91, 135.

14. Thysell, *Pleasure of Discernment*, 3. Early in the Reformation, Roman Catholics often used the term "Lutheran" to describe all Protestants.

15. Thysell, *Pleasure of Discernment*, 8. It was this decree that made John Calvin decide to leave France.

sister. The Roman Catholics plotted against her, but her rank gave her protection. Marguerite's pleading for others, though, no longer softened Francois, who grew more rigidly Roman Catholic.[16] Persecution of the French Reformed spread through the country, gaining strength. God had prepared Navarre in time to be a refuge; it became a safe haven for Protestants fleeing France. Believing clergy, highborn people, and common Protestants crossed the border.

Marguerite invited leading Huguenots to her palace at Nerac. At her table they discussed passages of Scripture; the queen was a delighted listener. Calvin and other Reformers found safety there.[17] Lefevre spent the last day of his life at her table. While the rest of the company was enjoying their meal, Lefevre appeared sad. Marguerite eventually drew out the reason. He said that he must die soon and face his Maker, and though he had lived a pure life, he had fled persecution and had never publicly left the Roman Catholic Church, unlike many who had followed biblical teachings and boldly come out for Protestantism, even at the cost of their lives. The queen comforted him, and he appeared satisfied. He then appointed her his executrix. When she asked what that would involve, he said, "The task of distributing my effects to the poor." She answered, "I accept the trust and it is more acceptable to me than if my brother had left me the whole kingdom of France." Lefevre then went to bed. He never woke up.

Like so many Reformed noblewomen of the time, Marguerite corresponded with Calvin. Appreciation of his work, thought, and counsel did not prevent the queen from taking offense when she felt the common-born pastor struck too close to home. She thought the "Treatise against Spiritual Libertines" was too harsh in its criticism

---

16. Bainton, *France and England*, 29.

17. Thysell, *Pleasure of Discernment*, 3. Many people found refuge there, including some with dubious theological positions. The Reformer Beza thought this was evidence of the queen's lapse into heresy after reading the writings of Marguerite de Porete, an author pushing the limits not only of gender roles but also of orthodoxy. Calvin saw the queen's condition as backsliding. Thysell, *Pleasure of Discernment*, 19, 21.

of certain men who had found refuge at Nerac, and she told Calvin so. He responded gently that he feared for her spiritual health with these men attending her in her court.[18] Though she was trusting in Christ alone for her salvation and did suffer for her belief, Marguerite remained in need of solid teaching.

In 1547 Francois died. Marguerite's grief was deep: "At this season of his cruel death, / Lord, I await your favour that I might hear good news."[19] The same year she published *The Triumph of the Lamb*, a lengthy poem discussing the fall, redemption, and consummation, particularly the person and work of Christ. It shows a greater familiarity with Scripture than her first published work, sixteen years earlier, did. She touches on so many Huguenot doctrines, from bondage of the will to predestination to the Lord's Day, that her movement toward Protestant orthodoxy since her conversion seems clear.[20] Christ's one-time sacrifice for the remission of sins is laid out:

It was not necessary to repeat
That offering to God; once was enough.
Were that not so, his death would be required
As often as a sacrifice was due.[21]

*The Triumph of the Lamb* is also much less of a journey of personal emotion and religious feeling; instead, the poem affirms scriptural truths as reality, focusing more on the reigning Christ than the saint's emotional response to salvation. Rich with Old Testament references, it is full of salvation's joy.

---

18. Thysell, *Pleasure of Discernment*, 9. Thysell believes that Marguerite's writings, prompted by Marie Dentiere, were in response to Calvin; the queen wanted a softer, more apparently unified Protestantism than Calvin advocated, presenting this "nuanced" perspective in her work *Heptameron*. Thysell, *Pleasure of Discernment*, 10–17. See Marie Dentiere, *Epistle to Marguerite de Navarre and Preface to a Sermon by John Calvin* (Chicago: University of Chicago Press, 2004).

19. De Navarre, "Song," in *Selected Writings*, 295.

20. Marguerite de Navarre, *The Triumph of the Lamb*, in *The Coach and the Triumph of the Lamb*, trans. Hilda Dale (Exeter, U.K.: Elm Bank Publications, 1999), 96–97.

21. De Navarre, *Triumph of the Lamb*, 107.

Marguerite's writing demonstrates an understanding of and love for biblical doctrine, as well as "a determination to show women engaged in contemporary intellectual discussions."[22] There is a deep, almost intuitive familiarity with Scripture's themes and passages:

> Encased in lambskin is the sacred Word
> Embossed with markings of a deep blood red,
> Sealed with seven seals may now be heard
> By those who find that law and grace are wed.[23]

No less thankful for her salvation and no less responsive to the gospel than at first, Marguerite seems to increasingly focus less on herself in her poetry and more on her Savior and His church.

Marguerite continued her quiet work of reform and protection until she died. Years before, she had written,

> O my God, that death is fair
> That takes me from this fetid air.
> By death I'm victor in the race.
> By death I look upon Thy face.
> By death I am to Thee conformed.[24]

Death made her faith sight. Some say that just before she died, Marguerite conformed to Roman Catholic rites, but her letters from the time are so evangelical that they exasperated the Roman Catholics and show her faith. She died December 21, 1549, rejoicing in hope and calling on Jesus to save her. Years before she had written,

> Faith gives hope of certain truth....
> I cannot fail to give thanks
> For the many undeserved blessings
> [God] deigns to bestow on his Marguerite.[25]

---

22. Broomhall, *Women and Religion*, 79.

23. Marguerite de Navarre, "The Primacy of Scripture," in Bainton, *France and England*, 21.

24. As quoted in Bainton, *France and England*, 26.

25. De Navarre, "Mirror of the Sinful Soul" in *Selected Writings*, 147–49.

She understood that her work was just a beginning: "God, I am assured, will carry forward the work He has permitted me to commence, and my place will be more than filled by my daughter, who has the energy and moral courage, in which, I fear, I have been deficient." Her dying hope was certainly fulfilled in her daughter, who bravely fought the battles for the Reformed, and in her grandson, who became king of France and gave the Reformed church the Edict of Nantes, which provided liberty of worship. So she laid a foundation on which her heirs could build, though she did not live to see it.

# 6

## Jeanne d'Albret

Marguerite de Navarre's only surviving child was Jeanne d'Albret. While Marguerite's protective work allowed the Reformation to take hold, Jeanne was its greatest military female defender. Marguerite knew her daughter's personality, and, as she was dying, spoke of the work that Jeanne might do for the church. Jeanne did not fail. With greater courage than her mother, she was fearless in her allegiance to and defense of the Reformation. Marguerite's faith was more private, working quietly and personally for reform. Jeanne's faith was public, total, and bold. Small and often ill, Jeanne was mentally intense, a firm believer in the divine right of kings—and queens. At the same time, she was unselfish; she lived for the Reformed church. She was prone to suspicion and anger and often appeared cold, but God used her tough personality for great good.

Born at the Chateau de Fontainebleau on January 7, 1528, Jeanne was raised in France away from her parents because Marguerite's brother, Francois I, king of France, wanted to control her. Without Marguerite at court and with religious divisions becoming more pronounced throughout Europe, Francois increasingly opposed the Reformation and even gave his approval of a Waldensian massacre in Merindrol. Surrounded by Roman Catholic influences as she grew up, Jeanne was not given the chance to be Protestant. But Francois soon found that she had a will of her own. The king of Spain had asked for Jeanne's hand for his son before she was even three months old; this arrangement was canceled when she was about twelve years old because Francois arranged a political marriage for Jeanne to the German Lutheran Duke William of Jülich-Cleves-Berge. The king was surprised when he found that Jeanne absolutely refused. Francois enlisted Jeanne's father and mother to help him persuade her, but all their influences, threats, and punishments—there were rumors of whippings—did not make her budge.[1] The king was immovable; she must marry the duke. So Jeanne did what she could: she drew up two protests against the marriage, stating that she was forced into it against her will, and had them witnessed and filed. In 1541, she was forced to go to the wedding ceremony. Refusing, Jeanne had to be carried to the altar, resistant to the end. The duke then went to war, and Jeanne was permitted to go home with her mother. God used a bad marriage to bring the stubborn princess into contact with the Reformed faith. Soon after, Francois and the duke turned against each other. Four years later the pope annulled Jeanne's marriage on the grounds of her documented protests and the lack of consummation. Jeanne was once again single, but now Protestant.

By her early twenties, Jeanne again attracted suitors, among them, the Bourbon prince Antoine, Duke of Vendome. She accepted him; from her side, it was a love match. He is known to have fathered illegitimate children and apparently married Jeanne for the opportunity to become king of Navarre.[2] The wedding was in October 1548, and the first years of their marriage were happy until Antoine's philandering and theology created a widening divide between them. Together, the couple had five children, but only two, Henri and Catherine, survived childhood.[3] When Jeanne's father died, Francois's heir wanted to annex her little mountain kingdom of Navarre; for the first time Jeanne revealed her ability as a stateswoman. She raised troops and prepared for war. Fortunately, before it came to battle, the French king died, and Navarre escaped the danger.

---

1. Jeanne's mother, Marguerite, initially protested Francois's actions but finally consented to the marriage. Thysell, *Pleasure of Discernment*, 13.

2. Roelker, *Queen of Navarre*, 80.

3. The third son apparently died when a nurse and manservant were tossing him back and forth and he fell from an open window and received fatal internal injuries. Roelker, *Queen of Navarre*, 102.

Under her mother's influence, Jeanne became more and more convinced of Calvinism. In fact, she became more convinced than her mother was and later came to see Marguerite's faith as plagued by hesitation and weakness. By 1559 she and her husband were queen and king. In December of 1560, Jeanne made an open profession of the Reformed faith before her people at her capital. Antoine, also claiming Protestantism, was not as keen—his motives were political.[4] But Jeanne's reforms would not be limited to having the Lord's Supper in a cellar or pleading for Huguenot prisoners. By 1563 her reforms included making Calvinism the official religion of Navarre, destroying or modifying Roman Catholic churches, banning Roman Catholic rituals, and banishing nuns and monks.[5] This was not sudden. Jeanne had been analyzing and planning for years, ever since her father's death. In 1555 she wrote to a friend, "A reform seems so right and necessary that, for my part, I consider that it would be disloyalty and cowardice to God, to my conscience, and to my people to remain any longer in a state of suspense and indecision."[6] The reforms were simply national expressions of deep personal conviction. "Calvinism," writes a biographer, "galvanized her energies and provided the unifying focus of Jeanne's life."[7]

The Roman Catholics could not ignore this activity. The pope sent letters of censure from Rome. On the Reformed side, Calvin sent letters of encouragement from Geneva. In France, Catherine de' Medici, Protestantism's most bitter enemy in that country, plotted against Jeanne.[8]

---

4. Bainton, *France and England*, 45.

5. Roelker, *Queen of Navarre*, 266.

6. Jeanne d'Albret to le Vicomte de Gourdon, August 22, 1555, in Roelker, *Queen of Navarre*, 127.

7. Roelker, *Queen of Navarre*, 153.

8. Catherine de' Medici (1519–1589) was born into the powerful Italian Medici family, married a son of Francois I, and became queen of France in 1547. From the time of her husband's death (1559) to her own, she held enormous power.

Antoine was then regent of France and had to be away from his wife for much of his time; his affairs became public knowledge, so that he was known as the playboy of the French court. Jeanne was more than heartbroken: "Although she has little power, I fear her anger," wrote one courtier.[9] She put her energy to good use in the capital, helping Beza establish a Protestant congregation with a functional consistory, publicly attending services, and giving the Reformed faith such positive publicity and support that many in Paris converted.

The Roman Catholics responded in kind. At the end of 1561, the Huguenot church began to experience increased persecutions. Prisoners were hanged instead of released; Protestant court tutors were fired; Huguenot property was destroyed. As the leading Protestant royal, Jeanne was under personal attack. Catherine de' Medici concocted a plan to separate Jeanne's husband from her, win him back to Roman Catholicism, and add the kingdom of Navarre to France. With Antoine on the lookout for personal advance and the Huguenots losing political clout, he was easy bait. Caught in the enemy's trap, Antoine renounced the Reformed faith. When Jeanne later visited Paris to bring her son, Henri, to Antoine, he treated her with contempt. With Catherine de' Medici, he tried to force her to go to Mass. But she would not be forced against her conscience, replying to the older woman, "Madam, if I at this moment held my son and all the kingdoms of the world in my grasp, I would hurl them into the bottom of the sea, rather than peril the salvation of my soul." Failing to gain outward conformity, Catherine and Antoine forbade Jeanne to hold private services—so she attended them at another Protestant noble's quarters. Husband and wife fought more and more over these issues, loud enough for others in the palace to hear.[10] Even in Geneva these tensions were common knowledge. When Jeanne became ill, Calvin wrote to her, "I know, Madame, that you are the prime target.... Do not fail to stand firm."[11]

9. Chantonay to Philip, September 4, 1561(?), in Roelker, *Queen of Navarre*, 163.

10. Roelker, *Queen of Navarre*, 180.

11. Jean Calvin to Jeanne d'Albret, March 22, 1562, in Roelker, *Queen of Navarre*, 182.

Jeanne's enemies plotted against her life; one of them urged that she be thrown over a wall into the Seine. Antoine and Catherine finally ordered her to leave France. Antoine took their son into his home and placed him under the care and teaching of conservative Roman Catholics.[12] As Jeanne parted from Henri, she shuddered at the thought of whom she was leaving him with, but there was nothing she could do. She made him promise never to go to Mass, saying that if he did, she would disown him.[13] He promised. Jeanne had a dangerous trip home to regain authority over her land of Navarre now that her husband was on the French side. With boldness, Jeanne led her little company of two hundred through enemy territory, recruits joining as she passed. The Reformed Duke of Conde garrisoned the city where she spent a night, preventing any attacks. On March 27 or 28, Jeanne fled to Navarre. She sent couriers ahead to call her soldiers for help; they met her halfway and escorted her safely to her own lands.

It was the first of her many hair-breadth escapes; instead of shrinking, she rose to the challenge, now realizing her danger and the full extent of the Roman Catholics' treachery. Her husband threatened her for introducing Protestantism into Navarre, but she did not flinch. A little while later, he lay dying from a bullet wound, cared for by a mistress. Jeanne found out too late to nurse him as she wanted to. It is said that he vowed to convert to the Reformed faith and promote the Augsburg Confession if he lived.[14] He did not survive. Until her death, Jeanne wore widow's clothes.[15]

As a widow, Jeanne had total power over her kingdom. While her husband was philandering in Paris, she had been alone. Now

---

12. Roelker, *Queen of Navarre*, 182.

13. Bainton, *France and England*, 54.

14. One of Antoine's last acts was to send Henri to stay at Montargis with Renee of Ferrera, so perhaps there was some truth to his claim. Roelker, *Queen of Navarre*, 203. By 1567, Henri was living in the French court again.

15. Bainton, *France and England*, 57.

she was free to rule without hindrance.[16] She solidified the reforms begun in 1561, forbidding Roman Catholic processions and licensing so many Calvinist preachers that they formed a synod by the fall of 1563. Despite the decrees against Roman Catholicism, Roman Catholic subjects plotted against Jeanne; dissent was something that plagued her rule. The French court employed the same cardinal who had broken Antoine's faith to write to Jeanne to try to talk her out of her zeal. Even if he had left out thinly veiled threats, Jeanne would have seen through it. She knew her enemy well: "I am ashamed of your throwing up to us the excesses on our side. Take the beam out of your own eye.... I will refrain from doctrinal discussion, not because I think we are wrong, but because you will not be brought to Mount Zion.... I know that Scripture is sometimes obscure, but when it comes to the Prince of Darkness, you are an example.... After you have repented I will sign [off] as your cousin and friend."[17]

The attacks continued. In the beginning of 1563, the French king suggested that Jeanne marry into the Spanish royal family. That failed. The same year, the pope issued a bull against her, demanding that she come to Rome or forfeit her lands to a Spanish prince. Jeanne diplomatically made the French court see the potential harm in allowing the pope to take foreign lands and redistribute them; the king and Catherine de' Medici became her intercessors on that point.[18] When the pope talked of disinheriting her family by declaring her marriage with Antoine void because of her previous marriage, she again used diplomacy to compel Catherine to prevent the pope from doing this and thus preserved Henri's right of inheritance. When the king of Spain started a rebellion in Navarre in order to draw Jeanne to it and then capture her, his own wife warned Jeanne of the plot. God made even Jeanne's enemies further her cause. In the fall of 1563, there was a plot to kidnap Jeanne and hand her over to the

---

16. Roelker, *Queen of Navarre*, 202.

17. Jeanne d'Albret to Cardinal d'Armagnac in Bainton, *France and England*, 61.

18. Henry M. Baird, *History of the Rise of the Huguenots of France* (New York: Charles Scribner's Sons, 1900), 2:141, 143.

Spanish Inquisition.[19] She escaped it, and despite poor health, every obstacle seemed to strengthen her faith. Finally, King Charles IX of France and the king of Spain together plotted to kill the Reformed, but especially Jeanne and the Prince of Conde.[20] Immediately, Jeanne gathered her forces and prevented the massacre—or at least postponed it for years, till St. Bartholomew.[21]

Now Jeanne's goal was to see her son, Henri, by this time thirteen years old. As a child, she herself had been taken away from her mother and raised in the same court; she wanted to get Henri out of France and under her Protestant influence. She was afraid he might become a Roman Catholic or succumb to alcoholism and the sexual immorality that had brought down his father in the godless French court. When she again visited France, she gained permission for her boy to accompany her as far as Vendome. Swiftly she planned his escape. A mistake would have been fatal. Jeanne secretly sent a messenger to her own court, telling them to have an armed force ready to meet her. Six hours after this courier left, Jeanne and Henri galloped for Navarre. The Spanish ambassador wrote, "[Jeanne] left here a few days ago. I have it on absolutely reliable authority that... she has taken both her children and all her retainers."[22] French authorities were not pleased.

---

19. Roelker, *Queen of Navarre*, 222–23.

20. Louis I, prince of Conde, was a French nobleman and Huguenot military leader. His gifts as a soldier enabled him at one point to capture Orleans and Catherine de' Medici.

21. The St. Bartholomew's Day Massacre, which began in Paris on August 23, 1572, and spread through other French cities into October, was the largely successful Roman Catholic attempt to crush Protestantism in France. The death toll is unknown, but modern estimates range from five thousand to twenty thousand total. Older ones range as high as seventy thousand. Taking advantage of Huguenots gathered in Paris to celebrate their prince's marriage, the massacre decimated Protestant leadership, marked a turning point in the French Wars of Religion, and caused an exodus of Reformed believers from France. The French Protestant church never regained the size or status it had before the massacre. Anne Marsh-Caldwell, *The Protestant Reformation in France* (London: Richard Bentley, 1847), 2:379.

22. The Spanish ambassador to Philip, February 19, 1567, in Roelker, *Queen of Navarre*, 241–42.

Jeanne arrived home safely. Now that Henri was in her court, she carefully trained him. He showed remarkable abilities, especially in the art of war. Her reforms in the nation continued.[23] Though Jeanne had slowed them down under political pressure in 1563, three years later she had banned dancing (seen as a racy pastime), gambling, prostitution, and more. Some Navarre leaders planned rebellion, which included kidnapping Jeanne and her children.[24] Once again she avoided the trap, and by 1571, Roman Catholic lands and buildings were confiscated.[25] When Henry VIII took over church lands in England, he had enriched himself and his friends. But Jeanne's similar actions were motivated by piety; she used all the resources from the confiscations to fund Calvinist churches, establish a seminary (which included paying the professors and supporting about one hundred students), create a public school system for boys, and a public elementary system for girls. Like other Calvinists, Jeanne was greatly concerned about education.

Rebellions, usually instigated and encouraged by French Roman Catholics, broke out again in Navarre. Jeanne was equipped to deal with them; rebellion seemed to harden rather than frighten her in her position.[26] Other issues proved to be more difficult. She was under huge personal and political pressure to come to Paris with her son, apparently to function as a go-between for the Huguenots in negotiations with the Crown. Seeing through the pretense, she dug in her

---

23. Along with the religious reforms noted here, Jeanne also put the country back in the black, replacing her husband's gambling and extravagance with thoughtful thrift. Despite this, because of rebellions and Antoine's creditors, Jeanne was usually in need of money and even mortgaged her jewels to keep the country's finances together. Roelker, *Queen of Navarre*, 260, 289.

24. Roelker, *Queen of Navarre*, 268.

25. Though she used every legal opportunity to end Roman Catholicism, Jeanne recognized that she could not control people's hearts in the matter, and Roman Catholics who did not hold public office and kept their faith private were permitted to continue living and working in her lands. Roelker, *Queen of Navarre*, 276–77.

26. Roelker, *Queen of Navarre*, 290.

heels in Navarre.[27] The military ability that God had given Henri proved valuable for his mother and his country; the next great war between the Huguenots and Roman Catholics, the third civil war (1568–1570) in the French Wars of Religion, was coming. Jeanne threw all her fortunes into this conflict. Although her mountain kingdom was not directly involved, Jeanne understood that defeat of the French Reformed would mean hardship for her kingdom, leaving it isolated between the aggressive Roman Catholic powers of Spain and France.

Jeanne left Navarre to save Protestantism in France. Afraid to tell her decision to her own councillors for fear they would prevent her, she stole away secretly and arrived at the port of La Rochelle, where the Huguenots had gathered for their defense. Her arrival astounded the city. The Reformed were thrilled by this unexpected reinforcement. The mayor presented her with the keys to the city. She was greeted with loud applause as she entered the Huguenot council. There, the Prince of Conde resigned his command of the Huguenot army into the hands of Jeanne's son. The audience responded enthusiastically, but Jeanne rose and graciously declined the offer. "No, gentlemen," she said, "I and my children are here to promote the success of this great cause or to share in its disaster. The cause of God is dearer to me than the aggrandizement of my son." She compelled Henri to decline the honor amid applause that showed the army would accept him as their leader, though he was just sixteen. When the Huguenots realized that Jeanne would not allow her son to lead their forces, they placed her at the head of the civil government as the governess of La Rochelle. She held the position for three years.

Despite the demands of her work, she had the New Testament translated into Basque, the vernacular language of Navarre, and published at her own expense. She had charge of all the correspondence with foreign princes, and it was her pleadings by letter that secured England's Queen Elizabeth as a Huguenot ally. History rates

---

27. Roelker, *Queen of Navarre*, 296.

Elizabeth I as a greater woman than Jeanne, though in character Jeanne was far stronger and godlier. But Elizabeth did help save the Huguenots by aiding La Rochelle with her fleet. The war was terrible, but Jeanne battled on. The kings of Spain and France plotted to seize Navarre while Jeanne was in La Rochelle, but she ordered it defended and saved.

Then came the Prince of Conde's death in battle on March 13, 1569, leaving the Huguenots without their beloved military leader. This so paralyzed the army that not even Admiral de Coligny could rally their courage. Despairing, he sent for Jeanne to come to camp, saying that she was the only one who had influence enough to inspire the army with courage again. She came before the army, with its flags draped in mourning. On one side of her rode Conde's son, Henri de Bourbon; her son, Henri, was on the other.

Then Jeanne made her best-known address:

> Soldiers, you weep. But does the memory of Conde demand nothing but profitless tears? No, let us unite and summon back our courage to defend a cause which can never perish and to avenge him who was its firm support. Does despair overwhelm you—despair, that shameful feeling of weak natures? When I, the queen, hope still, is it for you to fear? Because Conde is dead, is all therefore lost? Does our cause cease to be just and holy? No; God, who had already rescued you from perils innumerable, has raised up brothers-in-arms worthy to succeed Conde. To these leaders I add my own son. Make proof of his valor. The blood of Bourbon and Valois flows in his veins. He burns with ardor to avenge the death of the prince. Behold also Conde's son, the worthy inheritor of his father's virtues. He succeeded to his name and to his glory. Soldiers, I offer to you everything in my power to bestow—my dominions, my treasures, my life, and that which is dearer to me than all, my children. I make here a solemn oath before you all—and you know me too well to doubt my word—I swear to defend to my last sigh the holy cause which now unites us, which is that of honor and truth.

When she stopped, there was quiet for a moment, then shouts went up along the lines. The army hailed the young prince Henri as their leader.

There she stood before her army, inspiring her men. With de Coligny, Jeanne conducted the war. When the admiral was defeated and badly wounded at Moncontour, Jeanne set off to see him, despite the danger. She found de Coligny in bed, his jaw so badly shattered that he could not speak. Putting that defeat behind her, she planned for victory. Everywhere, her son's white plume became victorious until the Huguenot army camped outside the walls of Paris, forcing the Roman Catholics to make peace. Then Jeanne returned to her own kingdom, traveling through her lands, continuing to find ways of bettering her people's condition.[28]

But now the Roman Catholics determined to conquer by deceit, as they could not win in war. They laid the plans for the massacre of St. Bartholomew. Jeanne sensed deception, but she could not tell exactly what the danger was. De Coligny fell into the trap. The first step was to get Henri to marry the daughter of the French king Henry II and Catherine de' Medici. Jeanne objected. She did not want her son to marry a Roman Catholic. But all her councillors, with de Coligny at their head, favored the match. The Roman Catholics were so anxious to bring about the marriage that they agreed to a Reformed ceremony. Finally, forced by everyone around to give her consent, Jeanne went to Paris to make the necessary contracts and see that the rights of her land and religion were preserved. She opposed the French on many points, but they agreed to everything, so she finally signed the articles of marriage. Still she was not satisfied, feeling that there was duplicity somewhere. She did not know what was coming; she only felt it would hurt the Reformed.

Her anxieties proved too much for her. She became sick before the wedding on June 4, 1572. Her pain "continued to grow worse, 'but no word of impatience or complaint ever passed her lips.'"[29]

28. Roelker, *Queen of Navarre*, 385.

29. Smith to Burghley, June 7, 1572, in Roelker, *Queen of Navarre*, 388.

The Huguenots were dismayed at this illness; if Jeanne died, who would look after them? She comforted those around her bedside and in her last will and testament urged her children to remain true to the Reformed faith. When asked if she was willing to go and be with Christ, Jeanne answered, "Yes, much more willingly, I assure you, than to remain in this world where I see nothing but vanity."[30] She was mentally alert to the last and died quietly on June 9 at the age of forty-four.[31] "I have never feared death," she had said. "I do not dare to murmur at the will of God, but I grieve deeply to leave my children exposed to so many dangers. Still I trust it all to Him." She died with her Bible at her side, relying on its promises and receiving its crown.

Jeanne had unfurled her banners in the name of the Lord and of her Reformed faith, taking a front rank among the military leaders of her day. When her generals were killed, captured, or wounded, she rallied her troops to victory. She was never conquered in war. And she did not do it for herself but out of obedience to what she thought God had called her to: Protestant reform and protection of the Huguenot church. Everything was against her—the power of French Catholicism, lack of funds, an estranged husband, rebellious subjects, wars, poor health—but she persisted. She raised her son and daughter so that Henri later wrote of his "good mother, to whom I owe everything."[32] She also functioned as a mother to Protestant girls in Roman Catholic families.[33] Jeanne comes down to us

---

30. In Roelker, *Queen of Navarre*, 389.

31. An autopsy showed an abscess in Jeanne's side and some abnormalities in the brain but ruled out the possibility of poison, which many suspected. Marsh-Caldwell, *Protestant Reformation in France*, 2:301.

32. The daughter, Catherine de Bourbon, was like her mother in many ways: firm in the faith; married to a Roman Catholic; persecuted by the French court; offered refuge to Huguenot refugees (including Philippe de Mornay); and died prematurely. Death came quickly because of tuberculosis and an abdominal tumor, which Catherine believed to be a long-awaited pregnancy. Though she did not have her mother's political power, she was also faithful in her position. Bainton, *France and England*, 75–81.

33. Charlotte de Bourbon, who later became William of Orange's wife, owed much of her escape from Catholicism to Jeanne, who in the last weeks of her life

as one of church history's strongest female characters. She had seen great sorrows, but the greatest came after her death. The massacre of St. Bartholomew would have broken her heart, and so would have Henri's conversion to Catholicism. But she was gone. She died before defeat came, after a life of faithfulness. Years earlier she had said, "Although I am just a little princess, God has given me the government of this country so that I may rule it according to His gospel and teach His laws… I rely on God."[34] She could sing with Deborah,

> Thus let all Your enemies perish, O LORD!
> But let those who love Him be like the sun
> When it comes out in full strength. (Judg. 5:31)

---

worked on the young woman's behalf. Roelker, *Queen of Navarre*, 418. Jeanne also raised her husband's niece, Marie de Cleves, as a Protestant.

34. Roelker, *Queen of Navarre*, 216.

# 7
## *Charlotte Arbaleste*

Charlotte Arbaleste was born in Paris on February 1, 1548, into a prosperous family. Protestantism had been introduced to France years before her birth, but was still illegal. Charlotte's family reflected national religious tension: although her mother remained a Roman Catholic till death, her father converted in the later years of his life. Travels in Germany brought him into contact with Protestantism: at Strasbourg he heard a theological discussion between the Reformed and the Roman Catholics that opened his eyes to some of the abuses of the established church. But he did not understand or accept the gospel until years later, when the Roman Catholics charged him with heresy. At that point, still a Roman Catholic, he decided to examine what the Huguenots believed and believed it himself. His dying words in 1570 were, "Lord, you gave me a soul fifty-eight years ago.... I render it to you impure and polluted. Wash it in the blood of Jesus Christ, your son."

Despite her mother's Roman Catholicism and her father's late conversion, Charlotte seems to have believed at a much younger age. On September 28, 1567, she married the Protestant Jehan de Pas, seigneur de Feuqueres, and the next year gave birth to a daughter, Susanne. By 1569 Jehan was dead, and Charlotte was left alone with a toddling Susanne.[1] In 1570, Charlotte went to Paris to live

---

1. Charlotte de Mornay, *Memoires de Madame de Mornay* (Paris: Jules Renouard, 1868), 50, 57–58.

with her mother; she was still there when the St. Bartholomew's Day Massacre began.[2]

The morning the massacre began, a maid returning from an errand told Charlotte what was happening. Charlotte looked out the window and saw companies of soldiers with white crosses on their hats. A manservant went to her mother's home to find out what was the matter, and Charlotte then understood that her life was at stake. Three-year-old Susanne was sent to a Roman Catholic friend; Charlotte soon followed. She had hardly left her apartments when soldiers arrived. Angry that Charlotte was gone, they questioned her mother, then looted the home. For three days Charlotte, her daughter, and forty other Huguenots hid in a large Roman Catholic house; eventually something created suspicion, and soldiers were ordered to search it. The Protestants were warned, and everyone was able to flee except for Charlotte, Susanne, a maid, and one other refugee. Charlotte hid in an empty loft while the maid smuggled Susanne to Charlotte's grandmother. After the home had been searched, Charlotte escaped, hiding in different Paris houses for several days and under strong pressure from her mother to go to Mass, if only to save her life. Charlotte was "by the grace of God most determined in [her] refusal."[3]

She was staying in a room above a Roman Catholic lady's apartments and did not dare walk or light a candle in case someone heard or saw. When food came, it was a few bites hidden under an apron. On Wednesday, the eleventh day of the massacre, Charlotte determined to leave Paris at all costs. She found a passenger boat and boarded, finding that she traveled with two monks and a priest. At Tournelles, a guard demanded her passport. Charlotte had none; she was declared a Huguenot and sentenced right there to drowning. She begged to be taken to a gentleman in the city—a friend of the family who could vouch for her. Two soldiers brought her to the gate. Charlotte's friends assured the soldiers that she was harmless, so she was taken back to

---

2. Richard B. Hone, *Lives of Eminent Christians* (London: John W. Parker, 1850), 2:101.

3. Hone, *Lives of Eminent Christians*, 2:105.

the boat and allowed to continue her journey. But she was still in danger, as a group of soldiers were searching for her. The house where she had been staying was searched. She had escaped again.

Charlotte traveled to Villegrand where she stayed in the country with a vinedresser for fifteen days, then traveled from place to place, afraid that her presence would endanger her hosts and put her own life at risk. Finally she found safety with the Duke of Bouillon, who was also Reformed. During her stay, she used some money to pay the ransom of a prominent Huguenot soldier and statesman, Philippe de Mornay, who had been captured by the Duke of Guise. Like Charlotte, Phillipe had miraculously escaped the massacre despite being in Paris when it began. A devoted Huguenot, he had felt persecution for his faith even before St. Bartholomew's Day.[4] He became a frequent visitor in Charlotte's home; in 1575, he proposed and they were married January 3, 1576.[5] A well-known leader, Philippe married Charlotte for her character—she had no money or connections to attract him. In the following years, Charlotte gave birth to Marthe (1576); Elisabeth (1578); Philippe (1579); Maurice (1581), who died the same year; two stillborn sons (1583); a daughter (1586) who died as an infant; and Sara (1587), who died at three months.[6] A good mother, Charlotte grieved for her five dead children even as she cared for the surviving ones.[7]

The king of Navarre (who later became Henri IV of France) sent Philippe as an ambassador to England and Holland, and Charlotte traveled with him. Some of their children were born abroad. In addition to his political work, Philippe wrote several important Protestant works, contributed to the Edict of Nantes, and represented Huguenots

---

4. Hone, *Lives of Eminent Christians*, 2:88–90.

5. *Memoires de Madame de Mornay*, 83, 87, 102.

6. *Memoires de Madame de Mornay*, 111, 118, 124, 133, 146–47, 162, 165. Charlotte suspected that it was a hard journey during pregnancy that brought on the deaths of the two boys; perhaps the labor was premature. Regardless, it was a period of significant transition for the family and was stressful for the pregnant mother. Charlotte grieved the loss, though she knew it was from God's hand.

7. It seems as though Susanne was left to be raised by Charlotte's relatives.

at the Synod of Dort. His work was so essential to the formation of French Protestantism and beyond that some called him the Huguenot pope. Charlotte's support freed him to do much. She managed the household, discussed international politics and policy issues with him to help him with his work, and enabled him to fulfill not only his responsibilities on the job but also to contribute to the church.[8]

The family returned to Paris in July 1582, going from there to Montauban in southern France, the area most populated by Huguenots in the country. While there, an odd case of church discipline happened in the Reformed church. The local consistory was rigid about simplicity of dress, holding that according to 1 Timothy 2–9 and 1 Peter 3, Christian women should not curl their hair; it was prohibited on pain of exclusion from the Lord's Supper. Charlotte curled her hair anyway and was barred from the Table.[9] On his wife's behalf, Philippe spoke with the consistory, which did not budge. Charlotte replied to the consistory in writing, saying that they were the only Reformed church to take this stance: she had worshipped in German, English, Dutch, and other French churches and it had never been an issue. She also pointed out that Calvin's commentary showed that the passages referred more to vanity and pride in looks than to details of hairstyles, and that her own pastor had said from the pulpit that the gold and jewels "forbidden" in the same verses were God's creations and so acceptable to wear. The situation became more strained and more public, with Charlotte explaining church polity to the consistory as they pressed her harder: "I cannot understand how they call me rebel, given that I do not demand anything from them but that they show me the article in order to obey it. If there is one, they must not hide it from me, but if they turn the page, they will see article 26 that there is no power for ministers, consistories, colloquies, and

---

8. Broomhall, *Women and Religion*, 90–91.

9. It is sometimes easy to forget, when we look at portraits of godly women from centuries ago, that the sitters were often dressed in the latest fashions. Most of the women in this book wore their hair and clothes in styles that aligned with haute couture trends fitting for their stations in life. Godliness never has demanded frumpiness.

provincial synods to add, change or diminish [an article] without the advice or consent of the national synod."[10] She would submit, she said, if the elders could point to something in Scripture, the creeds, or confessions that gave local consistories power over parishioners' hair. Eventually, the family transferred to a different Reformed congregation that made no comment on Charlotte's coiffure.

This episode was not merely Charlotte being stubborn. She genuinely believed that the local church was overstepping its bounds and was willing to argue the point to keep her biblical freedom and clarify procedure. She could only do this with integrity because she knew her Bible and church polity. The fact that she was a woman in no way diminished her responsibility to understand the denomination's ecclesiology and to speak out when it was being abused. Frustrations with one consistory did not diminish her love for the church. In 1589 the family moved to Saumur. When the king converted to Roman Catholicism in order to take the French throne, he relieved Philippe of active service. He returned home to find that Charlotte had overseen and paid for the construction of a church building for the Reformed congregation. It was dedicated a few days after his return.

Her children's education also occupied her. She trained them in the hope that they would be useful to the kingdom. She had a son, then living in the Netherlands, to whom she wrote the following:

> My son, God is my witness that even before your birth, He inspired me with a hope that you would serve Him; and this to you ought to be some pledge of His grace and an admonition to perform your duty. Your father and I have also taken care to instruct you in every branch of useful learning, to the end that you may not only live, but also shine in His church. You are young, my son, and divers imaginations present themselves to youth, but always remember the saying of the

---

10. Arbaleste to the president of Clauzonne, April 1585, in Broomhall, *Women and Religion*, 42.

Psalmist, "How shall a young man direct his way? Certainly by conducting himself according to thy word, O Lord." Nor will there be wanting persons who will desire to turn you aside therefrom to the left hand or the right. But say also with the Psalmist, "I will associate only with those that keep thy laws. Thy laws, O God, shall be the men of my counsel."

The boy grew into a mature Christian—God's gracious answer to such prayers and admonitions.

This son's death in 1605, while fighting in battle for the Dutch, almost broke Charlotte's heart. She never recovered from the shock and survived him by only a few months. On Sunday, May 7, 1606, she attended the morning service and expected to go in the afternoon but became ill. She suffered greatly until the next Sunday, when her husband had to tell her that she would never recover. She received the news joyfully, saying, "I am going to God, persuaded that nothing can separate me from His love. I know that my Redeemer lives. He has triumphed." One of her doctors, a Roman Catholic, told her to take courage. She answered, "My courage is from above," and spoke to him of the biblical assurance that Roman Catholicism could not give, urging the man to look to Christ for his own salvation. The next day her pastor spoke Christ's words to her, "Father, into your hands I commit my spirit." She added words from Psalm 31:5: "You have redeemed me, O LORD God of truth." She died on May 15 with Jesus's name on her lips. When she was gone, Philippe said, "She assisted me to live well, and by her pious death, she has taught me how to die well." Earlier, a secretary had tried to sum up Charlotte's character. He wrote:

> There was no woman of her time more adorned with every kind of virtue. She had a clear understanding, a judgement uncommonly sound, courage which nothing could shake, and so great a detestation of vice, that even the most noble of her acquaintance feared to incur her censure. Besides this, her heart glowed with charity to the poor; and above

all, her zeal for the glory of God, and the advancement of his church, was ardent and conspicuous.[11]

Charlotte's contributions to the church, especially her support of her husband's work and trust in the midst of danger and grief, make her an example of female piety. Philippe was deeply grieved but continued working for reform until he followed his wife to glory seventeen years later.

---

11. As quoted in Hone, *Lives of Eminent Christians*, 107.

# 8
## *Charlotte de Bourbon*

For most of the sixteenth century, French kings belonged to the Valois dynasty. But the Bourbon family had members in line for the throne too; they were involved not only at court but also in military and religious action. Charlotte de Bourbon (c. 1546–1582) was the fourth daughter of the Roman Catholic Louis de Bourbon, Duke of Montpensier, and his wife, Jaqueline de Longwy.[1] The duke had financial difficulties that would have made it hard to provide suitable dowries for his five daughters, so he sent three of them to convents. The duke's friends highly commended his self-denying act in giving so many of his children to the church.

But while man makes plans, God directs the way. The duke never expected that his cloistered French daughter would become a Dutch Reformed princess. Charlotte was very young when she was sent to the convent of Notre-Dame de Jouarre in Normandy. At twelve or thirteen, she was made to take vows against her will; she drew up documents of protest and had them signed and witnessed by nuns

---

1. Good's account of Charlotte's childhood is that her mother was Reformed and secretly taught her daughters Protestant doctrine, praying for them when they were sent away. Unfortunately, he has no references. Broomhall has evidence that the mother wrote Charlotte harsh letters, commanding her to remain in the abbey against her will. Broomhall, *Women and Religion*, 30, 32–38. Bainton and other scholars identify the mother as Roman Catholic; she was a friend of Catherine de' Medici, actively served in the French court, and listened to Protestant ministers only in the last two years of her life. Certainly she could have had little to no influence on her daughter's theological perspective. The duke was part of the extended French royal family and never wavered in his loyalty to Rome.

who were sympathetic to her predicament. In 1563 or 1564, she became abbess. It was common in monasteries and convents to place those of high social status in such leadership roles, and Charlotte was of the royal Bourbon line. This "promotion" was also against her will, and she was so upset that she wept and could not speak audibly at the installation.[2]

While Charlotte grew up in the convent, the great struggle for Reformation began in France. Charlotte followed these developments with great interest; although a nun, she secretly sympathized with the Protestants. Being abbess, she had the opportunity to teach some Reformation doctrine to the nuns in her care.[3] Eventually, in 1571, Charlotte came under suspicion and was charged with spiritually perverting the nuns under her authority. She asked Jeanne d'Albret for advice. "Flee," was the answer. In February of 1572, Charlotte left the abbey with two nuns, giving the impression that they were visiting another abbey.[4] Instead, they headed toward Charlotte's sister, the Reformed Duchess of Bouillon, but because of continued danger, Charlotte went to Heidelberg, where Elector Frederick III of the Palatinate welcomed her as a daughter. Frederick, the same man who commissioned the production of the Heidelberg Catechism, was a known protector of the Reformed, opening his territory to them as a place of refuge. Shortly after her arrival in the city, Charlotte publicly renounced Roman Catholicism and sided with the Reformed church. She also publicized the fact that she had been forced into the abbey against her will, bringing out the protest she had signed years before.

Her father was still alive. When he heard of her flight from the convent, he was enraged. Wild rumors spread, speculating about her reasons for leaving despite her own confession of faith. Was there a lover involved? Had she run off with the abbey's valuables? With the

---

2. Bainton, *France and England*, 89; Broomhall, *Women and Religion*, 35–36.

3. There seems to have been a generational divide among the nuns; the younger ones were much more open to new teachings and were opposed to someone being forced into office against their will. Broomhall, *Women and Religion*, 36.

4. Broomhall, *Women and Religion*, 28.

rest of the family, the duke began a secret investigation, interviewing the nuns to find out why Charlotte had disappeared.[5] Eventually, the evidence became clear: Charlotte had been forced into the abbey against her will, but stayed to please her parents. Convinced of Reformed doctrine, under suspicion of heresy, and strongly encouraged by other Protestants, she had eventually fled.[6] But evidence did nothing to soften her Roman Catholic father.

Charlotte's flight was international news: "Such a high-profile defection was bound to be heralded as a victory for the Huguenots, and to need extensive justification by…the Catholic community."[7] The French court took the case, ordering that a search be made to find and severely punish Charlotte. At this, Elector Frederick wrote to the duke on March 15, 1572, notifying him that his daughter had found safety with him and that he had received her because she was guided by her conscience. This did not calm the duke. He was indignant that Charlotte had left the convent. If she had remained a Roman Catholic, he might have forgiven her, but her becoming a Protestant was too much. He went as far as to question Frederick's motives: "Can it be honorable for you to receive into your house children who have run away from their father? Is it not more worthy for you to advise them to return?" But Frederick did not flinch in his devotion to Protestantism and his protection of fellow believers; he answered Charlotte's father calmly, stating his willingness to return Charlotte, provided she was guaranteed freedom to worship in the Reformed way in France. Frederick wrote a similar letter to the French king, Charles IX. The king declared that he was willing to grant Charlotte freedom of religion and even appointed messengers to go to Heidelberg to bring her back, but the duke was inflexible: "If she means to persist in the Protestant religion," he wrote, "I would rather she would remain in Germany, than return to France to scandalize everybody, and be the misfortune of my old age." Charles's messengers

5. Broomhall, *Women and Religion*, 31.

6. Broomhall, *Women and Religion*, 30–38.

7. Broomhall, *Women and Religion*, 39.

came to Heidelberg, but Charlotte declined to go to France, as her father would not countenance her conversion. Originally, she had planned to travel to Navarre and live under Jeanne d'Albret's rule, but it was too dangerous.[8] So she remained at Heidelberg with the Palatinate court.

There she lived under Frederick's kind care. And there she met Prince William of Orange, who was on a visit to find military help in Germany. The two met in April 1572. She was a penniless, refugee nun; he was a wanted man with all of Catholic Europe against him. They decided to marry.[9] It might have been a suitable match on paper, for he was the ruler of the Netherlands and she was a princess of the French royal line, but the marriage was a brave step. It was necessary, for the sake of political peace, to get the French government's consent before the marriage could take place. The king refused to commit himself either way, so the Dutch court acted on the principle that silence gives consent, especially as Charles said he would raise no objections. The French government finally gave its consent. Other difficulties arose, but the marriage took place on June 24, 1575, in Antwerp. It was a very happy marriage: husband and wife were believers and had the same loves, goals, and hopes. Charlotte proved herself, as William's brother Johann said, to be "a wife distinguished by her virtue, piety, and intelligence." They were suited to each other, Charlotte being cheerful and helpful; "in return, he love[d] her tenderly."[10] By all accounts, William and Charlotte's relationship was unusually happy and harmonious.

But the marriage also brought cares and anxieties for Charlotte; her husband was fighting a deadly war with Spain. That country had done everything to defeat him and call into question the legitimacy of his marriage—William had separated from his second wife,

---

8. Bainton, *France and England*, 91.

9. Bainton, *France and England*, 99. William's marriage to Charlotte was his first Protestant marriage; he had converted from Roman Catholicism before they met.

10. Count Johann VI of Nassau-Dillenburg, as quoted in James Anderson, *Ladies of the Reformation* (London: Blackie and Son, 1858), 652.

who had been unfaithful.[11] The public reply that William circulated through European courts showed the Spanish king Philip II to be malicious, adulterous, and incestuous.

There were domestic cares as well. Charlotte cared for William's children from previous marriages: two boys and three girls, as well as a nephew and two nieces. She gave birth to six daughters between 1576 and 1581. The education of all the children was something Charlotte took seriously—which became evident later in their trained abilities. Often acting as secretary, Charlotte helped William with his administration. He gave her charge of all their Flanders estates, and she kept him up-to-date on domestic affairs whenever he was away. She also advised William and even acted as mediator when some of his subjects had a just complaint.[12]

In June 1580, Philip offered a large reward of twenty-five thousand crowns to anyone who would bring William, dead or alive, to the Spanish court. He denounced William's marriage to Charlotte in such terms that even her father became angry. The duke issued a document stating that the marriage—and the children—were legitimate and had his blessing.[13] Though thankful for this measure of family reconciliation, the Spanish aggression worried Charlotte, who did not enjoy good health. She was in constant fear for her husband's life: "Take care of yourself," she wrote to him in 1577, "I implore you to be more solicitous of your health."[14] Again and again she warned him to be careful, to avoid eating in public places, and not to let strangers approach him. But he had become so concerned with the good of the country that he was careless of himself in his work. He did not take Charlotte's warnings as seriously as he should have.

---

11. William's first wife, Anna of Egmond, died in 1558; in 1572 his second wife, Anna of Saxony, was arrested for adultery after years of unhappy marriage and alcoholism on her part. Her family continually raised objections to William's divorcing her, despite confessions of guilt from her and her lover and the birth of an illegitimate child. She died in 1577.

12. Bainton, *France and England*, 101.

13. Bainton, *France and England*, 104–5.

14. As quoted in Anderson, *Ladies of the Reformation*, 651.

On Sunday, March 18, 1582, what Charlotte feared happened. Two Spaniards, a master of a failing bank at Antwerp and his servant, plotted to take William's life. The servant was to do the deed, but the master was to share the reward. Before the servant, de Jauregui, went to kill William, a Roman Catholic priest absolved him of all sins and gave him Mass and a charm to protect his life. In case de Jauregui lost his nerve, the priest accompanied him to the castle and blessed his work as they separated. "Such," comments a historian, "is Jesuit morality...baptized murder."[15]

William had attended the Reformed church that morning and was at dinner with Charlotte, the children, and other members of the court when the assassin tried to enter the dining room. Servants prevented him. But after dinner William was showing a count some tapestry that depicted scenes from a war. De Jauregui again tried to force his way over; again the servants prevented him. William unsuspectingly rebuked the servants and ordered the man to be allowed to come, thinking that de Jauregui was merely a citizen who wanted to see him. Recognizing his opportunity, the assassin stepped forward, put his pistol over the count's shoulder, and fired. William was badly wounded in the head: the bullet entered under the right ear, passed through his palate, knocked out several teeth, and came out the left cheek. It grazed the jugular vein, cauterizing it. For a moment William did not seem to realize what had happened. Recovering himself, he asked that de Jauregui be spared, but he was already dead from multiple sword wounds at the hands of guards and other men. On hearing the shot, Charlotte rushed to her husband. Seeing him covered with blood that flowed from his head, she fainted. When she woke, she nursed William with great care. The wounds caused heavy internal bleeding. Ten days after the attack, the scab came off the jugular vein, creating more serious blood loss and threatening William's life again. By holding the blood vessel closed, Charlotte, other family, and servants were able to prevent William's death. By April 12, they

---

15. Anderson, *Ladies of the Reformation*, 657.

were sure of his recovery.[16] The Reformed people of Holland were deeply grateful that God had spared their prince and leader. On May 2 they held a thanksgiving service at Antwerp for his recovery, which both William and Charlotte attended.

But the period of care and anxiety before William's recovery proved too much for Charlotte. Almost immediately after the service, she collapsed and was carried to her deathbed. By May 5, 1582, she was gone. William had her buried in the beautiful cathedral of Notre Dame at Antwerp. Her story is a witness to the power of the Reformed faith. She became the ancestress of kings; her daughter married the son of Elector Frederick, who had so kindly shielded and befriended her when she was alone. Queen Victoria was one of her descendants. So a nun became a Reformed believer, a princess became the mother of kings, and a saint became a servant in heaven's court.

---

16. Anderson, *Ladies of the Reformation*, 661.

# 9

## *Louise de Coligny*

The great Huguenot admiral Gaspard de Coligny had four children:
Louise, born in 1555, was the eldest.[1] The admiral and his wife, Charlotte, gave their children a legacy of devotion to the Reformed faith.
They also gave them a quality education, hoping that they would not
only take hold of biblical faith but also be able to defend and advance
Protestantism. Both father and mother were serious about their faith,
privately and publicly, risking everything to defend the fledgling
French church. During her girlhood, Louise's father was busy with
the Huguenot wars, fighting and suffering for truth, but he made
time to write to his daughter. He encouraged her faith, reminding
her that the loss of earthly property and goods, even unjustly, was
not something to grieve if they had treasures laid up in heaven where
Roman Catholics could not take it.

Louise's beauty and gifts attracted suitors, and among them was
her father's emissary, Charles de Teligny, who had become part of the
Huguenot leadership despite his youth. He soon asked for Louise's
hand. Her father gave her this advice: "You have other suitors, rich
and titled, but I advise you to choose Teligny as your husband…on
account of the rare and good qualities which I know him to possess.
I give you this counsel, because I think it will contribute to your happiness in life, which we ought rather to seek in all things than great

---

1. "Louise" is the accepted spelling, although in letters, she signed her name
"Louyse." *Correspondance de Louise de Coligny Princesse d'Orange (1555–1620)* (1887;
repr., Geneve: Slatkine Reprints, 1970).

possessions and dignified titles."[2] Louise and Charles shared a double wedding ceremony with the bride's widowed father at La Rochelle in 1571, when Jeanne d'Albret, who was in attendance, was still ruling and the fighting had paused.[3]

The peace did not last long. When Henri de Navarre married Margaret of France, de Coligny went to Paris to attend the wedding, accompanied by de Teligny and Louise. An anonymous letter warned de Teligny about going, but, like his father-in-law, he was unwilling to be suspicious of others without hard evidence. At midnight, August 22, 1572, the church bell opposite the Louvre rang out the signal for the massacre, and thousands of Huguenots in Paris and beyond were murdered. Among the victims were Louise's father and husband. Her father was brutally killed in his room, his body thrown out a window onto the street as a sign of the Roman Catholics' success. Her husband managed to escape onto the roof with de Coligny's minister. De Teligny was so popular that one of the guards sent to kill him did not have the heart to do it, so the Duke of Anjou's soldiers carried out the order.

We do not know how Louise managed to escape the city, but she must have been alone and on foot. She made her way as quickly as she could to her father's castle in Chatillon in Burgundy to warn her stepmother and brothers to flee. Her escape was so rapid that she arrived before reports of the massacre. The news was like a thunderbolt to the family. But they had no time to mourn—only to run, and there was hardly time for that. They thought it safest to split up in their flight. Louise's two oldest brothers succeeded in escaping safely, as did her stepmother. With a cousin, Louise fled to Geneva. Her youngest brother was captured and taken back to Paris. So at seventeen years old, Louise was orphaned, widowed, exiled, and in poverty because the Roman Catholics had confiscated all her father's property. She stayed briefly at Geneva, moved on to Bern, and then

---

2. As quoted in Anderson, *Ladies of the Reformation*, 670.

3. Roelker, *Queen of Navarre*, 322.

Basel. The French offered to give back her family's property if she renounced her Reformed faith, but she preferred faithful poverty. The massacre had confirmed her opinions of Roman Catholicism, and nothing would induce her to trust its followers.

We know little of the next ten years of Louise's life. There is a story that Elector Frederick, the same one who had sheltered Charlotte de Bourbon, was involved in helping Louise in her exile. The Duke of Anjou, leader in the massacre, passed through Heidelberg on his way to Poland. The city ignored his unexpected visit; Frederick graciously allowed the duke to rest and eat in his castle. But politics did not prevent Frederick from bringing up uncomfortable issues. The elector was conducting the duke through the castle's portrait gallery when Frederick pointed to de Coligny's portrait and asked the duke if he knew whose it was.

"Yes," he replied, "the late Admiral."

Frederick became frank: "It is he, the best of men, the wisest and greatest captain of Europe, whose children I have under my protection, lest the dogs of France should tear them to pieces, as they have done their father." The duke felt awkward, but the elector continued: "Of all the lords of France whom I have known, that is the one I have found most zealous for the glory of the French name, and I am not afraid to affirm that the King and all France have suffered in him a loss that can never be repaired." The duke tried to apologize for de Coligny's death by suggesting that the Huguenots were forming a conspiracy at the time. Frederick cut him off, saying, "We know all about that, sir."

After William of Orange's third wife, Charlotte de Bourbon, died, William proposed marriage with Louise. He was content to have her without a dowry. She was happy to have a husband whose abilities and goals she could respect. They were married at Antwerp on April 2, 1583, and immediately took up their residence at Delft. The Dutch people were initially suspicious of a French bride but soon learned to love her. Louise was surprised by the simple manners and modest living of the Dutch, even in the upper classes, but came to appreciate or at least accept their customs. Her kindness made her many friends. One biographer says, "She was a small, well-formed woman, with delicate features, exquisite complexion and very beautiful dark eyes, which seemed in after years to be dim with unshed tears, with remarkable powers of mind and angelic sweetness of disposition." William's daughter Louise was pleased with her father's wife: "The new mother loves us all, and takes very good care of us."[4] Physically and mentally stronger than Charlotte, Louise was also an able wife for William, who found her to be a reliable counselor, loving wife, and capable mother. On February 28, 1584, she gave birth to a son, Prince Frederick Henry, who later inherited his father's title and position. The nation rejoiced at this birth.

Like Charlotte, Louise was afraid that William would be assassinated. Though the 1582 attempt had failed, Philip II still offered a large reward for William's murder. Louise's fears were well-founded; the man who would kill William was already in the palace. His name was Gerard, and he was a Frenchman from a part of France under Spanish control. Roman Catholic piety and hope of reward fed Gerard's plans for six years. He came to Delft in May 1584, took a position in William's service under a false name, and used money from William to buy pistols. Though Gerard had duped the prince, he aroused Louise's suspicions. She asked her husband, "Who is that sinister-looking man, and what does he want?"

"He wants a passport, and I will give it to him," the prince replied. After dinner, William left the dining hall and met Gerard in the hallway, at the foot of the stairs. Gerard held the passport in his hand, as though waiting for the prince to sign it, but his other hand held a pistol. The moment William turned his eyes away, Gerard sent three bullets through his body. The prince staggered under the mortal wounds and cried out in French, "O my God, have mercy on my soul and upon this poor people." One of William's ushers caught him and set him on the stairs. Louise and William's sister were at his side immediately. Realizing that he was dying, his sister asked him in

---

4. As quoted in Bainton, *France and England*, 118.

German if he commended his soul to Christ. He answered yes, his last word. Servants carried him to a bed where he died immediately. It was July 10, 1584.

Louise was overcome with grief. At thirty-two she was twice widowed. The violent death of this husband painfully brought back the assassination of her first husband. With an eighteen-year-old Maurice taking William's place of leadership, Louise now had a greater burden of advising and educating. Throughout the ordeal, she trusted God and bore her sorrow in a godly way. "She had," says one biographer, "the advantage to be sprung from the greatest man in Europe, and to have had two husbands of very eminent virtues, the last of whom left behind him an immortal reputation. But she likewise had the misfortune to lose them all three by hasty and violent deaths, her life having been nothing but a continuous series of afflictions, able to make any sink under them. But a soul like hers had resigned itself entirely to the will of God."

William's assassination happened a little over two years after the first attempt; Louise was a widow after fifteen months of marriage left with a collection of stepchildren, her own six-month-old, and no income. "I hardly know," she wrote to her husband's brother, "how the children and I are to maintain ourselves according to the honor of the house."[5] But the Dutch provinces kindly granted her a yearly allowance of twenty thousand francs. So God provided for the rest of her life.

But William's death meant that Maurice was now at the head of a country still at war with Spain.[6] In 1685, the Spanish advanced against the struggling Dutch, taking over important towns and putting the country at risk so that Queen Elizabeth I sent troops, under

---

5. After William's assassination, Louise wrote to his brother several times, saying that her children had no other father and asking for his help. Louise de Coligny to Jean de Nassau, July 26, 1584, in *Correspondance de Louise de Coligny*, 8; see also 9–14.

6. William's oldest son, Philip William, had been taken to Spain to be raised as a Roman Catholic. The Spanish plan worked, so the Protestant Netherlands recognized Maurice as William's successor.

the command of the Earl of Leicester, to help the Protestants. Unable to help in battle, Louise worked behind the scenes, writing the earl on several occasions and using the secretary to the British Privy Council as a messenger.[7] The alliance successfully pushed back the Spanish, leading to a treaty in August of that year. It gave Louise some reprieve from the intensity of the conflict, though her activity did not diminish.

She spent time building international connections with the British and French and often writing letters to the Dutch Estates General and the secretary of state. Maurice received letters from his stepmother, who addressed them to "my son" and advised him as she had advised his father.[8] Louise also had to focus on the extra responsibilities she now had at home.

The education of William's daughters from previous wives was now Louise's job. Some of them lived with other relatives; Louise kept five of them at home.[9] She took charge of the girls' education herself and worked faithfully to instruct them. It was said she so stamped her own character on them that many of the stepdaughters resembled Louise in character more than their mothers. Louise's pastor took over Frederick Henry's education until Maurice made the boy his apprentice in military matters.[10] As the children came of age, Louise helped with marriage arrangements, then took interest as grandchildren arrived.[11]

France was never far from Louise's mind, and even after decades away from it, she was still homesick. Most of her married

---

7. Robert Dudley, Earl of Leicester, was a defender of the Puritans in England and morally supported the Calvinist Low Countries as a friend of William the Silent and then as a benefactor of Maurice. *Correspondance de Louise de Coligny*, 22–24. See also her other letters to Leicester, 27–30, 36–41.

8. *Correspondance de Louise de Coligny*, 55, 56.

9. Bainton, *France and England*, 120.

10. Bainton, *France and England*, 120. Louise also had advice from Philippe de Mornay, at her request, on raising a son. Louise de Coligny to Plessis-Mornay, July 1591, in *Correspondance de Louise de Coligny*, 95, 263.

11. Bainton, *France and England*, 122.

stepdaughters lived there.[12] While living in the Netherlands, she had stayed informed about the religious situation in France. Henri de Navarre became king of France in 1589, making it safe, then legal, for Huguenots to live in the country. Louise chose to return home in 1598.[13] Not everything had changed: on a Sunday of that year, she happened to meet the Duchess of Montpensier, who had distributed badges to Roman Catholics who had taken part in the St. Bartholomew's Day Massacre. She was still a respected member of the French court. When Louise realized who the woman was, she explained why she could not stay in the room and abruptly left.

The French situation had calmed down, but controversies broke out in the Netherlands between the Calvinists and the Arminians. Louise moved back to the Netherlands in 1603 and lived in The Hague. There she founded a French Reformed church and had as her pastor a man who became a leader of the Arminian party. Whether it was this man's teachings, grief at more violent unrest, or personal conviction, Louise became associated with the Arminians. "She ranked herself," writes a biographer, "on the wrong side, but no doubt she acted conscientiously."[14] The rift between Calvinists and Arminians grew deeper, and in 1617 Louise wrote to Philippe de Mornay, asking for his "wise advice" on the situation. She was worried about the state, her children, and the church.[15] The split was intense and threatened to divide the country. An Arminian sided with Spain in order to oust and replace Maurice.[16] When the Dutch

---

12. She corresponded regularly with many of her stepdaughters, especially the Duchess of Thouars, Charlotte Brabantina, whom she called "dear daughter" and "daughter of mine." See, for example, *Correspondance de Louise de Coligny*, 221, 248. Letters to her grandchildren also survive. The letters communicate not only day-to-day information about the family but also discussions and advice about international religious and political issues.

13. Bainton, *France and England*, 124.

14. Anderson, *Ladies of the Reformation*, 695.

15. Louise de Colligny to Du Plessis Mornay [*sic*], December 28, 1617, in *Correspondance de Louise de Coligny*, 309.

16. Bainton, *France and England*, 131.

government ordered all the Arminians, or Remonstrants, to leave, Louise interceded for them, especially for her pastor, in the interests of religious freedom. She was on the losing side. Disagreements with Maurice made her less welcome in the country. So in 1620, Louise moved back permanently to her native France.[17]

Her son, Frederick Henry, later became the Dutch ruler and reintroduced religious freedom. So she ultimately gained the victory for her principles. But before this happened, she had passed to her reward. She lived only a short time after her second return to France. At Fontainbleau Palace she became sick. When news of the seriousness of her illness got out, the Roman Catholics tried their best to win her back to their faith. Cardinal Richelieu, hard and manipulative, was sent to do it. When he entered Louise's room, he found a Reformed pastor on one side and a Protestant friend on the other. Richelieu said, "Madam, take care of your soul. You have two evil spirits beside you." And then he professed deep anxiety for her spiritual condition, urging her to save herself by returning to the Roman Catholic Church. But the cardinal who shaped French history found his match in this dying Reformed woman. She was not de Coligny's daughter and William of Orange's widow for nothing. Though unhappy with the division between Calvinists and Arminians, Louise was a strong believer. She declared herself unshaken in the principles of the Reformed faith and in her hope of heaven through Christ's merits, and asked to be spared his intrusion. Richelieu left defeated, and her pastor comforted her with Christ's all-sufficiency till she died at sixty-seven years old on October 9, 1620. Her will stated that she commended her soul to God and to His Son, Jesus Christ, having lived and wanting to die in the Reformed religion.[18]

---

17. Her move home was actually delayed because her living arrangements fell through; she asked her stepdaughter the Duchess of Thouars to take care of it for her, which she must have done soon after Louise wrote in March. *Correspondance de Louise de Coligny*, 330.

18. "Testament de Louise de Coligny," in *Correspondance de Louise de Coligny*, 333.

In her will, she kindly provided for many of her servants and believers in various Reformed churches. Protestants of every brand grieved her death. Her body was embalmed and taken to Delft and put in a magnificent tomb with her second husband. Through her son, Frederick Henry, she became the great-grandmother of William III of England, who would carry on Reformation work in his native Low Countries and in Great Britain.

# 10

## *Katherine Willoughby*

Born in 1519 or 1520, Katherine Willoughby began life in high social circles. Her mother was a lady-in-waiting to Henry VIII's first wife, Catherine of Aragon; her father was a wealthy English noble. Her father died when she was young, and she was made a Crown ward. At the time, it was customary for the king to sell wardships to the English aristocracy; those who purchased Crown wardships had to pay for their ward's expenses but also gained any income generated by the ward's lands until the child came of age. The king's good friend Charles Brandon, Duke of Suffolk, purchased Katherine's wardship.[1] He was married to Henry's younger sister Mary, who took great care of Katherine's education.

When Henry VIII wanted a divorce and separated from Rome, Brandon declared himself a Protestant, the only safe thing to do. But his religious position seems to have been pragmatic: "His only demonstrable ecclesiastical enthusiasm was for church music," and he "showed little sign of theological commitment."[2] We do not know when Katherine was first exposed to Reformed theology or when she was converted, but it was likely during this time of religious change in the Tudor court.

In 1533 Mary died; within nine months her son, Katherine's intended husband, was also dead. So Brandon married Katherine,

---

1. Brandon and Mary Tudor were Lady Jane Grey's maternal grandparents.

2. Stephen Gunn, *Charles Brandon: Henry VIII's Closest Friend* (The Hill Stroud, Gloustershire: Amberley, 2015), 118, 120. See also 131, 176–77 for Brandon's pragmatist approach.

keeping her valuable lands in the family.[3] He was forty-nine; Katherine, around fourteen. To us, this age gap seems criminal, but at the time it was not unheard of in the upper classes, and the marriage appears to have been peaceful.[4]

A duchess now, Katherine's increased social status had brought her in closer contact with the royal family: she and her husband hosted the king and his fifth wife in their home; she reached out to a lonely Princess Mary, Henry VIII's oldest daughter; and one of her sons was friends with Prince Edward.[5] Katherine was also good friends with Henry's sixth and final wife, Catherine Parr, who married Thomas Seymour after Henry VIII died. The former queen died shortly after giving birth to a daughter, so Katherine cared for the child. Katherine also saw that some of the former queen's devotional writings were published.

In 1539 the duke hired Alexander Seaton, a Black Friar turned Reformer, as his chaplain.[6] Brandon still held "no strong religious views," but his wife had "an unusual interest" in church matters.[7] If Seaton did not introduce Katherine to Reformed theology, then his biblical preaching strengthened her spiritual condition. She became increasingly Reformed in her convictions, which soon became public. Already called "virtuous, wise, and discreet," Katherine later became known as one of Protestantism's fearless publicists.[8]

---

3. Gunn, *Charles Brandon*, 146.

4. It was Brandon's fourth marriage; the death of Princess Mary left him without income from her lands and reduced his movable property, such as jewels. Gunn, *Charles Brandon*, 152–53. Despite two apparently happy marriages, Brandon had illegitimate children.

5. Gunn, *Charles Brandon*, 234.

6. Seaton had fled Scotland, then under Roman Catholic rule, for England; though he was under the duke's protection, he still suffered interrogations and suspicion of heresy by Bishop Gardiner until his death in 1542. Foxe and Knox both commend him in their writings as a faithful and godly man. D. Hay Flemming, "Alexander Seaton," in *The Original Secession Magazine* (Edinburgh: James Gemmell, 1886), 17:78. Also spelled "Seton." Gunn, *Charles Brandon*, 175.

7. Gunn, *Charles Brandon*, 175.

8. Countess of Rutland, as quoted in Gunn, *Charles Brandon*, 189.

Katherine had a sharp wit, which she sometimes used to target her opponents. The enemy who impacted her life most was the Roman Catholic Bishop Gardiner. Unlike the king and the duke, who both used religion for personal and political ends, Gardiner was ideologically driven, fighting reform even from prison.[9] Principles, position, and power were things he had in common with Katherine, whose own strong ideological drive pitted them against each other. Both were clever, but Katherine did not have the political or manipulative bents that the bishop, who was known for his diplomatic skill, had, even though he could resort to more straightforward methods of fighting when diplomacy failed.[10] Biographers tell of one dinner party where it was announced that each lady present should choose the gentleman she loved best to take her into dinner. Katherine quickly spoke up: since she could not go in with her husband, whom she loved most, she would go with Bishop Gardiner, whom she hated most.[11] At one point, she apparently had a dog she named Gardiner, and she dressed it up in purple robes. These things rankled. Gardiner did not hide his hatred of Katherine; her rank and close relationship to the royal family did not prevent him from trying to charge her with heresy. He publicly opposed her and her Reformed faith. Katherine's friendship with Henry's last queen offered protection. There was an attempt at one point to arrest Gardiner, but nothing came of it.[12]

Brandon's wealth in land, buildings, and cash increased thanks to his friendship with the king, who was selling former Roman Catholic holdings at bargain prices.[13] Despite being in perpetual debt, Bran-

---

9. G. Constant, *The Reformation in England: Edward VI, 1547–1553* (New York: Sheed and Ward, 1942), 348.

10. Constant, *Reformation in England*, 226–28.

11. In his book of martyrs, Foxe describes many of Gardiner's persecutions against the Protestants. John Foxe, *The Acts and Monuments of the Church…* (New York: Robert Carter & Brothers, 1856), e.g., 617, 863.

12. Rumor had it that Brandon led the attempt, but he was not in London when it happened. Gunn, *Charles Brandon*, 211.

13. See, for example, Gunn, *Charles Brandon*, 208.

don often had the means to add to his holdings, which brought him more than three thousand pounds in annual income.[14]

In 1545 Brandon died, leaving Katherine a widow with two sons.[15] She was in her midtwenties. Widowhood brought a reduced income but also reduced expenses, and Katherine's annual income was thirteen hundred pounds—enough to live comfortably even while paying off her husband's debts. In fact, she was one of the richest women in England at the time. Included in her inheritance were many buildings and movable property, such as jewels and valuable horses.[16] Educating her sons became one of Katherine's great cares; she had them sent to Cambridge and was thoughtful about the men from whom they learned. One of their professors was Martin Bucer, whom she personally cared for in his last illness out of thankfulness for his work in the church.[17] Both sons were proving themselves capable in their callings, with promising marriages before them, when they died within an hour of each other of the sweating sickness in 1551.[18]

Left without family in the years after her husband's and sons' deaths, Katherine's personal faith grew stronger and, with Edward VI on the throne, became very public. Perhaps her husband's death freed her to be open. Henry VIII's death certainly made things easier for Calvinists: Gardiner was in prison, the prayer book was more biblical, and England became a Reformed nation. In 1550 Katherine

---

14. Three thousand pounds was a significant amount in the Tudor era, though Henry VIII was taking in far more than that every year at the time of his break with Rome. Contemporary examples of priest's incomes show that fifteen pounds per annum was desirable. Laquita M. Higgs, *Godliness and Governance in Tudor Colchester* (Ann Arbor, Mich.: University of Michigan Press, 1998), 78.

15. Charles was so close to the king that Henry had him buried in the chapel royal at Windsor Castle.

16. Gunn, *Charles Brandon*, 221, 235.

17. Anderson, *Ladies of the Reformation*, 332. Bucer had come to minister in England at Cranmer's invitation.

18. This disease no longer exists and we know little of it, aside from symptoms recorded by Tudor doctors which indicate that it was probably not viral. It was contagious and highly fatal.

began helping Protestant refugees from Europe. Bainton writes that in the same year, she hosted John Foxe, who became famous for his *Actes and Monuments*, when he came to London for ordination.[19] But the Reformer Hugh Latimer became her primary spiritual influence, serving as her chaplain from 1551 to 1552.[20] Under his teaching, Katherine's biblical knowledge and faith grew. When the number of refugees in London reached into the thousands, Katherine used her political connections and resources to obtain a charter that allowed them to establish a recognized church, the only congregation in England to legally exist outside of the Church of England.[21]

In 1553 Katherine got married for a second time to Richard Bertie. Brandon had been rich, political, old, nominal, and noble. Bertie had little money, was devoted to reform, was one year older than Katherine, and—it shocked everyone—was one of her servants. Though his father had been a manual laborer, Bertie had worked hard, graduated from Oxford, and gained a good position in a noble home. But it seems to have been his piety and ability in directing her affairs that attracted Katherine. Bride and groom were very happy, and Katherine signed over valuable property to her husband exclusively, making him landed gentry and softening the effect of her scandalous choice.

During this marriage, Katherine's faith would be tested in new ways: in July 1553 Edward died, and Mary, a devoted Roman Catholic, took the English throne. As the new queen entered London, she passed the Tower and freed Gardiner, making him her Lord Chancellor.[22] "Bloody" Mary expelled from the country the refugees Katharine

19. Bainton, *France and England*, 257. The book is commonly known as Foxe's *Book of Martyrs*.

20. Latimer's *Fyrste Sermon* was dedicated to the duchess and bore her coat of arms. Bainton, *France and England*, 256–57.

21. Called Charter of the Church of the Strangers, the document was a rare exemption under Edward VI from the Act of Uniformity. Jasper Ridley, *Bloody Mary's Martyrs: The Story of England's Terror* (New York: Carroll & Graf Publishers, 2001), 36–37.

22. Ridley, *Bloody Mary's Martyrs*, 44–45.

had helped and informed Roman Catholic authorities in their home countries of their deportation, which ensured their arrest.[23]

When the persecutions began, Katherine sent money to prisoners, including Bishop Ridley, so that they could buy food and clothing.[24] When Mary reestablished the Mass in the Church of England, Katherine determined not to attend. Her rank was no protection, especially as her old enemy, Bishop Gardiner, held so much power. Knowing that Katherine had no fear for herself, her enemies attacked her through her husband. Gardiner ordered Bertie to be arrested and sent to London without bail. The local official allowed Bertie to stay at home until his court date, Good Friday, with a payment of one thousand pounds. When he reached London, Bertie was interrogated by Gardiner on at least two separate days—the bishop feared that dealing with heretics on Good Friday was not the best use of the holy day. Pretending to be upset about an old debt that was paid off during Edward VI's time, Gardiner tried to extort four thousand pounds from Bertie. Losing the money would not only have set the couple back financially, it would also have hindered Katherine's support of other Protestants. But Bertie's legal right was easily established, so before letting him go, Gardiner touched on the real issue: Katherine's refusal to attend Mass and the bishop's bitterness against her because of her tireless support of the Reformation. Pressing him to make his wife return to Roman Catholicism and making veiled threats, Gardiner let Bertie go.

Because the couple realized they were in serious danger, they decided to flee England. Bertie managed to convince Gardiner that he was leaving in order to collect money that Charles V owed to Katherine's first husband, and the bishop secured a license from Bloody Mary that allowed Bertie to leave and return to England as often as he needed to until his business was finished. He left home and made secret plans for Katherine to flee as well. Traveling with

23. Ridley, *Bloody Mary's Martyrs*, 51–52.

24. Anderson, *Ladies of the Reformation*, 338.

their one-year-old daughter, Susan, and seven low-ranking servants, a pregnant Katherine left her London home early one morning before light, dressed as a servant. One of the higher-ranking manservants in the house heard a noise and began following them; Katherine sent the servants ahead to a quay along the Thames, hiding with two maidservants and the baby until the manservant returned home. Through someone—perhaps the manservant—the bishop got news of their flight and sent people to Katherine's home to see if she was there and to take inventory of her belongings. Finding the report of her flight true, Katherine's enemies tried to prevent her from leaving the country, searching inns and boats in likely ports. In a port town, Katherine and her daughter stayed under false names and met up with Bertie until they could sail. The bishop's men arrived and wanted to search the boat that Katherine had finally boarded, but a faithful servant put the bishop's men off the scent by convincing them that the woman was a merchant's wife. So the family and their servants made it safely to the Netherlands, where so many of Queen Mary's victims fled. Once again, a biographer comments, Katherine had "out-Gardinered Gardiner."[25]

The couple landed in Brabant, a duchy ruled by the Lutheran William of Jülich-Cleves-Berg, Jeanne d'Albret's first husband. In 1555, while they lived in the town of Santon, the local authorities and a bishop suspected that the couple were hiding their identity and decided to examine them. Bertie and Katherine fled. It was February; the ground was frozen and rain fell heavily as the couple walked with their little girl and two servants to the next town, Wesel. After three or four hours on the road, they arrived, but everyone refused them shelter, suspicious of the circumstances and the large amount of money that the couple offered for a room. Bertie spoke little German and sheltered his family near the doors of the church while he tried to find someone who spoke English, French, Italian, or Latin. Hearing two schoolboys speaking Latin, Bertie asked them to take his

---

25. Anderson, *Ladies of the Reformation*, 347.

family to a place where they could spend the night; the boys brought them to a friendly house where they stayed for several days and were taken care of. Word of their difficulty finding shelter spread around the town. That Sunday, a local preacher rebuked the people from the pulpit for their lack of hospitality. Rumors spread that high-ranking English Protestants were living in Wesel; more English Reformed people fleeing persecutions arrived. Under Katherine's patronage, they established an English church.

In October Katherine gave birth to a son, Peregrine. The entry of the boy's birth and baptism in the church records makes it clear that Katherine's identity was an open secret: "the most illustrious Lady Katharine, Baroness of Willoughby, Duchess of Suffolk, in the kingdom of England."[26] A month after the boy's birth, Gardiner died in England. His successor was just as dangerous, however, and it was impossible for the family to return home. Queen Mary's agents realized where the couple was and did all they could to force them back; Mary's Dutch ambassador informed Bertie that the Crown would confiscate his properties and goods if he did not return and claim them. The House of Commons vetoed this; Katherine's enemies maneuvered politically to march Austrian troops through Wesel, seizing the couple en route. Tipped off by the same ambassador, they fled into the Palatinate. It was a temporary refuge. Husband and wife were both glad to receive an unexpected invitation from Jan Łaski, whom they knew from his stay in England, to come to Poland where they would be safe. The trip began in April 1557. Interrupted by an attack by soldiers and a civil dispute that saw Bertie briefly jailed, the family finally arrived in Poland. The authorities there welcomed them, even giving Bertie the governorship of a Polish district.

Despite their safety in Poland, the couple's time there was brief. In 1558 Queen Mary died; Elizabeth was crowned on January 15, 1559. Katherine wrote the new queen a letter of congratulation,

---

26. Anderson, *Ladies of the Reformation*, 353.

expressing her joy and thankfulness that the English were now free to worship biblically. The family made for home.

Katherine spent the last years of her life supporting the reconstruction of English Protestantism. She supported all Protestants, including dissenters and other Christians outside the Church of England, interceding for ministers who preached without a government license.[27] Having been fruitful when free and faithful when persecuted, the duchess died on September 19, 1580. Her husband died a year and a half later; their children carried on their parents' faith.[28]

---

27. Bainton, *France and England*, 275–76.

28. Peregrine Bertie remained friends with the duke's former chaplain and inherited his mother's family's lands and the title Lord Willoughby. Gunn, *Charles Brandon*, 214, 225.

# 11
## Renee of Ferrara

The Reformation spread into Roman Catholicism's heartland, Italy. There, a woman helped introduce Protestant doctrine and protected those who followed it. The Duchess of Ferrara, sometimes called Renee of Este or Renee of France, was the patroness of Italian reform. French by birth, she was born at the Chateau de Blois on October 15, 1510. Her parents, Louis XII of France and Anne of Brittany, had earnestly prayed for a son and heir to the French throne. So when another girl was born, they were disappointed. Some historians described her as ugly, even a hunchback—reports that do not match surviving portraits.[1] Regardless, her childhood was difficult: by her fifth birthday, both her parents were dead and her governess was banished from the court; while she was a young teenager, her older sister Claude died in her arms.[2]

These difficulties did not stop Renee's academic progress. Marguerite de Navarre, whose brother married Renee's sister, Claude, oversaw the princess's education.[3] She managed to make Lefevre—

---

1. Renee's sister, Claude, queen of Francois I, suffered from scoliosis, which made her spine curved and her body hunched. Perhaps Renee also shared the disease and portrait artists ignored it, or perhaps some historians confused the two women. Barton claims that one of Renee's legs was shorter than the other and that one shoulder "protruded." F. Whitefield Barton, *Calvin and the Duchess* (Louisville, Ky.: Westminster John Knox Press, 1989), 12. Throughout her life, Renee suffered from migraines.

2. Barton, *Calvin and the Duchess*, 10–11.

3. Holt N. Parker, introduction to *The Complete Writings of an Italian Heretic*, by Olympia Morata, ed., trans. Holt N. Parker (Chicago: University of Chicago Press, 2003), 7. Marguerite was Louis XII's cousin.

famous for his early reform work and Scripture translations—Renee's tutor. Renee excelled in languages, classic literature, and even mathematics, but most of all, she began reading the new Protestant theology.[4] Likely, she was converted during her stay with Marguerite and Lefevre at Nerac.[5]

Renee's noble birth brought early marriage. She nearly married the young prince who later became Emperor Charles V. Then came the Duke of Bouillon, one of the richest men in France, and Cardinal Woolsey, asking her hand for England's Henry VIII, to succeed Catherine of Aragon. But on May 28, 1528, when she was only seventeen, she married the Roman Catholic Ecrole II d'Este, Duke of Ferrara.[6] The duke's mother was the infamous Lucrezia Borgia, who, among other things, has been accused of murder and sexual immorality; the duke's grandfather was the philandering Pope Alexander VI. Although it was a political marriage that was intended to strengthen French ties with northern Italy, Renee went to Italy to be a faithful wife in a family that hardly knew what that was.

Her husband's court was a cultural center in Renaissance Italy, with a highly intellectual court circle connected with the university, known beyond Italy for its wealth and learning. The court artist was Titian; the scholar Bernardo Tasso became Renee's secretary. But Renee never liked Italy and never even learned to speak Italian, though she was capable and could have received instruction in it.[7] She brought her own servants, ladies-in-waiting, and Protestant governess.[8] Though she lived in Roman Catholic Italy, she remained

---

4. Bowles, *Olympia Morata*, 34.

5. Barton, *Calvin and the Duchess*, 12.

6. Older works refer to him by his anglicized name, Hercules. His son and successor, Alfonso II, was the last Duke of Ferrara, and in 1570 the area, including the palace, was severely damaged by earthquakes. Bowles, *Olympia Morata*, 19, 21.

7. Parker, introduction, 8.

8. This governess, Michelle de Saubonne, was a highly educated noblewoman who had overseen Renee's education. She was a Calvinist and went with Renee to Italy as a mentor, friend, and teacher for her future children. The Protestant poet Clement Marot, who also spent time in Renee's court circle, knew de Saubonne, whom he

true to her Reformed religion. And like other Protestant French princesses, she spent money on what she thought was important: clothes, servants, alms, and education. Her husband complained about the expense: they were essentially paying for two separate courts from one ducal income.

As early as 1528, there had been a Reformed minister at Ferrara, but we do not know whether this was because of Renee's influence. She did not trumpet her Reformed activity but worked steadily for the Protestant church. For her children—Anna, Alfonso, Lucrezia, Eleonora, and Luigi—she initially found Protestant tutors.[9] Her husband's chief physician, Manzolli, was Reformed.[10] Some of the professors and many international students at the University of Ferrara were also Protestants. Clement Marot, the Reformed hymn writer, stayed in Ferrara with Renee for a time.

In the spring of 1536, John Calvin arrived in Ferrara, using the alias Charles d'Espeville. The duke thought he was another French scholar come to enjoy the intellectual climate in Ferrara. The Reformer Theodore Beza, a close associate of Calvin, observed that the duchess realized what was really happening: "When the Lady Duchess of Ferrara saw and heard Calvin, she knew of whose spirit he was; and as long as he lived, she remained for him a special instrument of God, faithful in love and devotion."[11] Calvin gave Renee a copy of his newly published *Institutes of the Christian Religion*. Whether it was Calvin's influence or simply her personality, Renee was down-to-earth in her theology, never taking on the mystical tone that some of her friends did.

---

included in his work "Epitre a Madame da Soubize" [*sic*], written around 1536. Marot uses a different form of the woman's full name, which was Michelle de Saubonne, Madame de Soubise. Henry Morley, *Clement Marot and Other Studies* (London: Chapman and Hall, 1871), 1:78.

9. Bowles, *Olympia Morata*, 57–59.

10. Manzolli's works, which satirized the vicious life of the clergy, were forbidden by the pope; after Manzolli's death, his body was disinterred and burned for heresy.

11. As quoted in Barton, *Calvin and the Duchess*, 5.

For a number of years, Renee had freedom in her religious efforts and welcomed many refugees from France, saving hundreds from starvation as they traveled. This cost her husband money, and some argue that Renee, lonely in Italy, received these people simply because they were French. It is true that she felt a burden of care for people who would have been her subjects if she had been male, but Italians also found her kind: "The poor and sick were sure of relief—orphans of care and protection: so that, in the whole city of Ferrara, there was scarce a person who could not shew some instance of that unlimited goodness."[12] She was not as staunch and open in her faith as other Reformed princesses, but she was no closet Protestant. A king's daughter had more liberty than most women, but the time came when she drew the attention of the Inquisition. Renee aroused the suspicions of the Roman Catholic clergy—and of her husband.

Though Ecrole was a Renaissance man and promoted the new humanism, he was a Roman Catholic. Despite his broad-minded approach to art and science, his religion made him increasingly intolerant of any dissent. In 1536 he made an agreement with the pope that forced the exile of all French Protestants from Ferrara: governess de Saubonne was sent home.[13] A young Protestant servant who publicly made fun of the Mass was arrested and tortured, despite the duchess's intercession. Persecution crept into Ferrara, and husband and wife became open enemies. Renee wrote to Marguerite de Navarre, "I am sure that Madame de Soubise has told you of the terrors and even assaults made against me since she left. I cannot bear any more. Without the help of the Lord I could not have. Daily my vexations increase."[14] Without encouragement, teaching, and support from Calvin, Renee might have given in then. She did not realize that trouble was only beginning. Calvin's support was a spiritual lifeline for the Italian Reformed community.

12. Bowles, *Olympia Morata*, 38.

13. Thomas McCrie, *History of the Progress and Suppression of the Reformation in Italy in the Sixteenth Century* (Philadelphia: Presbyterian Board of Education, 1842), 79.

14. As quoted in Barton, *Calvin and the Duchess*, 7–8.

In August 1542, Renee helped the Reformer Bernardino Ochino escape a death sentence in Italy and reach safety in Geneva.[15] This went beyond kindness to other Frenchmen or personal conviction; Renee was interfering with Italian politics and going against Rome. Both her husband and the pope were annoyed.

In 1543, Ecrole wrote to the French king, complaining that Renee had refused Mass, been religiously "seduced by some Lutheran rascals," called the Mass an idolatry, and refused to let priests near her teenage daughters.[16] The same year the pope visited Renee, trying to buy her allegiance by giving her a valuable diamond and other jewels. The bribe did not work. In fact, it seems as though Renee's actions became more decided, countering her husband's work. He refused to allow refugees in Ferrara; Renee funded escapes. The duke filled his prisons through the Inquisition; Renee visited those in chains. The little Reformed congregation at Ferrara dwindled until 1550, when it went underground; Renee was the only known Protestant left in Ferrara. The Inquisition surrounded her with spies, but Renee corresponded with Reformed friends, especially Calvin. In a letter to Marguerite de Navarre, Renee mourned her utter isolation.

Having destroyed her church and friends, the Roman Catholics now turned to destroy her. About 1552 Rome sent a Jesuit inquisitor to assess Renee's heretical condition; he found her to be a better debater than he was and reported that she was obstinate. Unsuccessful in converting Renee, the Jesuit demanded that the duke exclude her from all society. Her children were taken away, all Protestant servants were replaced, and any Protestants were barred from visiting. They even took her books. Renee was allowed conversation only with the Jesuits, who worked to brainwash her. Calvin wrote, trying to

---

15. McCrie, *History of the Progress*, 182–83. He was not the only pastor whom Renee helped to escape. Celio Curio and others reached safety because of her boldness. McCrie, *History of the Progress*, 188, 203.

16. Duke of Ferrara to Henry II in Bainton, *Germany and Italy*, 241–42. Lutheranism seems to have reached Italy before other brands of Protestantism, but Calvinism was clearly strong as well.

guide and strengthen her under the persecution. Threatened, abandoned by anyone who could help, and prey to fears, she weakened. Her love and fears for her children led her to try to see them again: in 1554 she received the Mass in exchange for access to them.[17] Jesuits boasted of her conversion to Rome, and her husband gave her more freedom, though she never lived with him again.[18] In 1559, the duke died, bequeathing Renee a fortune as long as she remained a Roman Catholic. But Renee's faith was not dead. She again spoke out for her Reformed religion. She was given the choice of converting or leaving Italy. She left for France, warned against the move by the pope and Calvin, who each had their reasons for thinking it unwise.

France had changed during Renee's thirty-year absence. Her old friends were almost all gone, and the political situation was significantly different. Renee found herself tied to various groups and factions in the court: her daughter Anna had married the Roman Catholic Duke of Guise; Renee was friends with Jeanne d'Albret; she enjoyed Admiral de Coligny's friendship; and she never rejected Catherine de' Medici's acquaintance. In trying to maintain neutrality on a personal level, she found herself in a position that did not satisfy anyone.

Though she did not ally herself politically with the Huguenot church or give them military support, Renee offered Huguenot refugees protection when she was able. She interceded for them with Catherine de' Medici; corresponded with England's Elizabeth I, pleading for them; and encouraged Jeanne d'Albret. Determined to relieve the suffering caused by the Wars of Religion, Renee retired to her ancestral lands around Montargis. The castle became an asylum for the persecuted Reformed; they called it *Hotel Dieu*—God's Hotel. In it, Renee sheltered crowds of people; it is said that one time, three hundred sat down at her table for a meal. Her compassion was not limited to the Huguenots; others suffering because of war, Italian refugees, and even monks found help in Renee's domain.[19]

---

17. McCrie, *History of the Progress*, 207–8.

18. Bainton, *Germany and Italy*, 243.

19. McCrie, *History of the Progress*, 242; Bainton, *Germany and Italy*, 246.

The townspeople of Montargis, though, were largely committed Roman Catholics. They loudly protested Renee's attendance at the Huguenot church. Knowing their violence, she held services in her castle. But a Roman Catholic mob attacked the Huguenot church during worship; the Protestants responded by trying to desecrate a Roman Catholic graveyard. The Catholics rioted in front of the castle but were sent away. Finally, the Roman Catholic Duke de Guise, Renee's son-in-law, determined to destroy that "nest of heretics" at Montargis, and ordered Renee to leave her home. He sent General Malicorne, who threatened that if she would not deliver up the castle, he would batter it to pieces and put her Reformed ministers to death. Renee's blood boiled: "Malicorne," she said, "take care what you undertake. There is not a man in the kingdom that can command me but the king. If you attempt what you threaten, I shall place myself first upon the breach, that I may find out whether you will be audacious enough to kill a king's daughter.... I have the means of making the punishment of your temerity felt by you and your offspring, even to the very babes in the cradle."[20] "This decrepit, prematurely-old woman," says a writer, "cowed the general with six companies of soldiers at his back." Malicorne left. Doubtless, Renee would have been driven out of her castle for another reason, but soon after this, the Duke of Guise was assassinated, and Montargis was safe.[21] As it was, Renee was forced to send away hundreds of refugees but provided them with transportation and food for their journey.[22]

Renee's interest in the church extended to her attendance at consistory meetings and even participation in them. Her Genevan pastor, Morel, complained about this to Calvin; Calvin rebuked her, kindly reminding her that Paul forbade women to exercise ecclesiastical authority. She replied that the queen of Navarre, Admiral de Coligny's wife, and the Prince of Conde's mother-in-law had done

---

20. As quoted in Baird, *History of the Rise of the Huguenots*, 2:110.

21. Renee's daughter Anna married another Roman Catholic duke who also fought against the Huguenots.

22. Bainton, *Germany and Italy*, 247.

the same thing, but she would stop. Calvin also helped her work through personal issues; when her Roman Catholic son-in-law died and she was hurt by Huguenot preachers saying that he was in hell, she discussed her thoughts with Calvin. Pastoral encouragement from Geneva was a mainstay for Renee throughout her life. When Calvin died she grieved greatly. His regard for her was so great that he wrote to her from his deathbed. She cherished his memory with great veneration.

The awful Massacre of St. Bartholomew may have changed Renee's mind about the nature of French Catholicism. Her greatest sorrow was that her daughter, the former Duchess of Guise, was involved in the politics behind the slaughter. With her usual kindness, Renee protected and saved many Huguenots in that massacre.

On June 12, 1575, Renee died at Montargis and was greatly mourned by the Huguenots. Only the church valued her legacy; all five of her children converted to Rome, despite her efforts to teach them biblical truth. At her death, Roman Catholics destroyed any of her correspondence that they could find.[23] Her tomb is in her castle, with the arms of Ferrara and her cipher topped by a crown. On one side of the inscription are the lilies of France, and on the other, royal ermine. Renee's uncertainties and weaknesses, though they may have prevented her from increased service, did not stop her from loving those around her nor prevent God from using her to protect His church.

---

23. As stated, Anna married the French Duke of Guise; Alfonso inherited his father's title and position; little is known of Lucrezia; Eleonora had an unhappy marriage; and Luigi became a cardinal. Little of Renee's correspondence survived; other records in Roman archives were also lost. Parker, introduction, 18.

# 12

## *Olympia Morata*

While the Reformation spread through northern Europe, the Renaissance boomed in Italy. Ferrara and Florence were centers of intellectualism and art; in Rome, the pope patronized painters, sculptors, and architects. Into this neoclassical humanism, Olympia Morata was born. While she is best known for her intellectual abilities, it is her faithfulness in suffering that makes her legacy so valuable for the church.

Her father, Fulvio Pellegrino Morato, was teaching in Ferrara when Olympia was born in 1526 or 1527.[1] He left the court for several years when Olympia was young, opening a school in Vicenza and carefully educating his own children. During this time, his religious views seem to have been changing; we don't know when he was converted, but this period was at least one of theological reexamination. In 1539 the family returned to Ferrara, where Morato became a tutor in the court and taught at the university.[2]

Olympia had other tutors besides her father—Italians and Germans who were experts in everything from languages to Copernican astronomy.[3] She must have been a quick learner; by the time she was twelve, her academic abilities were internationally known. At fourteen, she lectured publicly in Latin, wrote a defense of Cicero, and was known for her abilities in Greek and her understanding

---

1. Parker, introduction, 3.
2. Parker, introduction, 6.
3. Parker, introduction, 11–14.

of Homer's poetry.[4] Olympia became so academically polished that when Renee wanted an academic companion for her daughter Anna, she chose Olympia. The teenage scholar went to live with the princess, where they spent their days reading Aristotle, Ovid, Euclid, and even Erasmus—everything from philosophy to geography to languages and poetry.[5] It was a pleasant time for Olympia, who loved the studies, enjoyed writing, and found court life stimulating.

While Olympia was living in the palace, the brief Italian Reformation bloomed. We know little of her father's conversion, but he was closely associated with a Calvinist group.[6] At the court, Olympia still idolized the classics. She says of herself, "I had no taste for divine things. The reading of the Old and New Testaments inspired me only with repugnance." At one point Olympia tried to reconcile Christianity and the classics but later looked back on this period as one of spiritual indifference.[7] Renee's impact and Calvin's stay strengthened the evangelical influence in Ferrara, but it was Olympia's father's change from a concern with classical humanism to love for Christ and the Protestant church that most influenced her, and at some point she also began to love Christ and His church.

Morato became seriously ill in 1546; Olympia left the court to nurse him. As Morato waited to die, he bore a beautiful testimony for Christ. His death in 1548 was the beginning of Olympia's many sorrows. The same year, Anna, to whom Olympia had been a teacher and friend, left Italy to marry the French Duke of Guise. With no royal, Roman Catholic advocate, Olympia had no defense against the suspicion of being a Protestant, which was perfectly true. The former favorite of the court's social circle, she was now forced out: accused of Protestantism, prohibited from reading the Bible, and forbidden fellowship.[8] After the duke dismissed her, she went to live with her

---

4. Parker, introduction, 16.

5. Parker, introduction, 10.

6. Bainton, *Germany and Italy*, 253.

7. Bainton, *Germany and Italy*, 254.

8. Bainton, *Germany and Italy*, 255.

invalid mother, three sisters, and young brother. Like Moses, she chose to suffer with God's people rather than recant her faith and enjoy the pleasures of a godless court. A family friend noted that Olympia "took over the running of the household and gave her brothers and sisters an honourable education."[9]

Olympia still wanted to study for herself, but now she read the Scriptures. Among those who had come to study at the University of Ferrara and spread reform in Italy was a German, Andrew Grunthler, who knew of Olympia. Grunthler "admired Olympia's singular erudition and chaste morals; she in turn respected a man who had no bridal present other than talent."[10] He asked for her hand and was accepted. A friend of the groom wrote that Olympia chose him "so that she could more easily devote herself to sacred literature."[11] They became husband and wife in 1549 or 1550 and were "joined together in a beautiful marriage."[12] The prayers of the little Reformed church of Ferrara went up for God's blessing on the young couple. Olympia, twenty-four years old, wrote a hymn on the occasion, arranged like a Greek ode but with Christian content:

Wide-ruling Lord, highest of all rulers,
Who formed the male and the female sex,
You Who gave to the first man a wife for his own,
    lest the race die out,
And wished the souls of mortals to be the bride of your Son
    and that He die on behalf of His spouse,
Give happiness and harmony to husband and to wife,
    for the ordinance, the marriage bed, and wedding are yours.[13]

---

9. Caelius Secundus Curio to Sixtus Betuleius, Basel, December 25, 1550, in Morata, *Complete Writings*, 62.

10. Curio to Betuleius, in Morata, *Complete Writings*, 62.

11. Jakob Baldenburger to Joachim Vadianus, Basel, November 20, 1550, in Morata, *Complete Writings*, 63.

12. Curio to Betuleius, in Morata, *Complete Writings*, 62.

13. Olympia Morata, "Wedding Prayer," in *Complete Writings*, 181.

But danger gathered around the little Reformed church of Ferrara, which Olympia called "my ungrateful city."[14] The Duke of Ferrara and the pope worked to wipe out the Protestant church in Italy. So Grunthler prepared to return to Germany, looking for a job and a place to live. He left Olympia behind, afraid that a winter journey over the Alps would be too severe for her. He returned several months later to get her. Starting in May or June 1550, with Olympia's eight-year-old brother, Emilio,[15] they traveled through the Tyrol, passed the imperial army, and arrived at Schwaz, then Augsburg and Wurzburg.[16] Olympia's fame preceded her in Augsburg; the Fugger brothers, who were wealthy merchants, welcomed her, and the couple enjoyed their stay. In Wurzburg, Emilio had an accident: while playing with a friend, he fell head first from a tall gallery onto rocks below. Those who witnessed the fall thought he was dead, but he was not at all injured. Olympia said she saw in it how God gives His angels charge over those who are His saints. One of the aspects of German life she enjoyed was the availability of Protestant books; she sent some of Luther's writings back to friends in Italy.[17]

An invitation came for Grunthler, offering him the position of personal physician to the Archduke of Austria, Ferdinand I.[18] The couple agreed on their response. Declining the archduke's offer, Olympia wrote: "I think it is hardly unknown to you that we serve under Christ, and that we are bound with an oath to His military

---

14. Olympia Morata to Lauren Schleenried, c. January 1553, in *Complete Writings*, 130.

15. Olympia's three sisters were all in service to noblewomen, one of them in the household of Livinia della Rovere, a believing Italian woman whom Olympia considered more intelligent than she was. Morata, *Complete Writings*, 115–16.

16. Parker, introduction, 26.

17. Bainton, *Germany and Italy*, 261.

18. Ferdinand became Holy Roman Emperor in 1558, and Grunthler's talent was well known. There was also a social connection: Ferdinand's daughter married Renee of Ferrara's son.

service, so that if we abandon it we will pay an endless penalty. . . .
We would be sinning against God."[19]

By the end of 1550, the family reached Schweinfurt, Grunthler's
hometown, where he had secured a position as doctor to the many
soldiers stationed there. So Olympia, the great classic scholar, came
to live in a quiet country village. She used her training to educate her
brother and translate many psalms into Greek. The couple enjoyed
the kindness of the local Protestants, especially the pastor. Olympia
kept up her correspondence with German and Italian friends as well
as theologians like Melanchthon. She also wrote a few poems, which
she called her children: "I think I have to give the answer to one
question you asked me, whether I had given birth to anything. The
children I bore on the very day and hour I received your letter, I am
sending to you.... I have borne no other children, and so far have
no expectation of bearing any."[20] This infertility seems to have been
a quiet grief for Olympia, and she does not often mention it, though
she regularly showed interest in her friends' children. Caring for her
younger brother probably helped ease the pain. Initially, the couple's
time in Schweinfurt was quiet.

But in the end their place of refuge was the place of greatest danger. War swept the town. Albert of Brandenburg, fighting Emperor
Charles V, happened to choose Schweinfurt as the place in which to
defend himself. In April 1553 his army occupied the village and forti-
fied it while the emperor surrounded it.[21] A siege began and lasted
fourteen months. The small family had to face all the awful reali-
ties of war. Artillery battered town walls and houses. Civilians were
afraid to go outside but sometimes died in their homes. Bands of
the enemy would sometimes enter the town, force themselves into
houses, and take what they wanted. Famine added its horror to violence, and disease followed famine, until half of the population was

---

19. Olympia Morata to Hormann's son, 1552, in *Complete Writings*, 127.

20. Olympia Morata to Caelius Secundus Curio, October 1, 1551, in *Complete
Writings*, 116.

21. Parker, introduction, 29.

gone. In all this, Olympia's courage did not forsake her. She wrote, "Under the weight of so many evils we have found consolation only in prayer and meditation upon the holy Word." Her husband caught a fever and seemed to face certain death, but God answered Olympia's prayers and Grunthler recovered "without any medical intervention."[22] This gave her courage. The Lord who had spared her husband would certainly care for them in the siege.

Conditions grew worse. The townspeople's bravery angered the enemy. A rain of fire came down on the town at night. Houses gave no safety; people were forced to go underground. Olympia, with Grunthler and Emilio, spent several weeks in a wine cellar, afraid to go out. Finally, on June 12, 1554, Albert of Brandenburg saw that defeat would come if he stayed and suddenly evacuated the town in the middle of the night. Enemy troops entered the next day but brought no relief, only worse oppression. They pillaged Schweinfurt, then set it on fire. The people pressed to the gates for escape, only to be driven back. Some made their own funeral preparations at home. Some fell on their knees, begging in vain for mercy. Others crowded in the church as a place of safety, only to die as the building collapsed in the fire. Olympia and her family were drawn into the crowd that was surging toward the church where they would have died, when an enemy soldier told them to flee or be buried under the ashes of the town. They left their home with nothing. As they looked back, they saw the flames shooting into the night sky and the houses crackling under the heat. The fire consumed most of Olympia's writings. Their money and beloved books were gone. They hurried on.

Outside the city a band of soldiers attacked, plundered all they had, and took Grunthler prisoner. Olympia had no money for ransom, so they let him go. Somewhere along the way they were stripped of their clothes and left in their undershirts. During that awful night they traveled more than ten miles in the dark, barefoot. In her great distress Olympia cried to the Lord, "Help me, help me,

---

22. Olympia Morata to Caelius Secundus Curio, July 25, 1554, in Morata, *Complete Writings*, 139.

for the love of Your name." She had lost her shoes and most of her clothing, her hair was disheveled, and she was ill with malaria.[23] Olympia later wrote that when they arrived at the village of Hammelburg she looked like a beggar queen, entering emaciated, feverish, in a borrowed shirt, and utterly exhausted. She remembered, "I was barely able to crawl there."[24] The citizens of Hammelburg did not dare keep her long for fear of the local Roman Catholic bishop, who had ordered that all refugees be put to death. Once more, enemy soldiers captured and then released Grunthler. She likely contracted tuberculosis during this time in addition to the malaria.

They worked their way into the Palatinate, to the Duke of Erbach's estate. Safe at last, Olympia broke down completely. Her fever raged. But a count and his family tenderly cared for her. The countess gave her the love of a sister, and when she began recovering, Olympia was thankful to find that Emilio's heart was opening to the Reformed faith. Perhaps this was due to the influence of the count's family. The count had daily family worship and often visited his people, exhorting them to piety. He used his influence to have Grunthler appointed as a professor at Heidelberg, and an unknown nobleman gave the couple money, perhaps for travel expenses. When they were about to leave, Olympia collapsed again and was ill for four weeks.[25] After her recovery, the family again made their way to a new home. It was Olympia's last.

They arrived at Heidelberg in August 1554 and enjoyed it. The city was not only a beautiful place; it had also become a center of learning. There, Olympia even found a former Greek teacher who welcomed them. On hearing that the family's books had been destroyed, several publishing houses sent replacements. Money was still an issue, so Grunthler borrowed twenty gold florins to pay for their first month of living expenses. While her husband lectured on

23. Bainton, *Germany and Italy*, 265.

24. Olympia Morata to Caelius Secundus Curio, July 25, 1554, in Morata, *Complete Writings*, 139.

25. Morata, *Complete Writings*, 144.

medicine, Olympia attended to things at home, noting that while housework kept her busy, "we always carry those domestic enemies with us—sin and the old Adam."[26] Just as she had throughout her life, Olympia kept up a large correspondence, often urging her readers to study the Word, even if it meant they had to get up a little earlier in the morning. Sadly, she often felt as though nobody answered: "It's amazing how many letters I write but no one writes me back."[27]

The destruction of the little Reformed church of Ferrara distressed her. Some of its members were imprisoned, some were exiled, and others had fled. Renee's temporary apostasy caused Olympia pain. Her companion Anna of Este was married to the duke who so terribly persecuted the French Reformed. Olympia wrote to Anna. After asking after Anna's health and telling her about her husband, Olympia described her own salvation. She pleaded with Anna on behalf of the Protestants: "You know, my sweet princess, how many innocent persons now are burned and crucified for the gospel of Christ. Surely it is your office to speak up on their behalf. If you are silent, you conspire in their death."[28] The charge must have touched Anna's conscience. Though she remained firmly in the Roman Catholic Church, Anna was the only one in the French court who dared voice opposition to the persecutions.

Olympia was also busy educating Emilio. She taught him the classics but especially loved to open the Word to him. That was her consolation in those days of poverty and weakness. Though she had little time for reading herself and missed her mother terribly, Olympia and her husband were finally safe in Heidelberg. But Olympia was not permitted to live long in this peaceful home. Her sufferings during the siege at Schweinfurt and her flight weakened her so

---

26. Olympia Morata to Lavinia della Rovere Orsini, August 1, 1554, in *Complete Writings*, 142.

27. Olympia Morata to Vittoria Morata, August 8, 1554, in *Complete Writings*, 146.

28. Olympia Morata to Anne, Duchess of Guise, in Bainton, *Germany and Italy*, 262.

that she never fully recovered, and in June 1555, plague broke out at Heidelberg. By July Olympia had become so weak that her life was despaired of. She felt that she would not get well. Writing to a friend she said, "As for me, I grow weaker day by day. The fever never leaves me for an hour."

Her death was radiant with hope. A few hours before she died, she woke up and smiled. When asked why, she said, "I, in a dream, saw a place illumined by the purest, most beautiful, brilliant light."

Her husband answered, "Courage, my well beloved; you will soon dwell in the midst of that pure light." She smiled and nodded assent.

Soon after that, her sight failed. "I can see no longer," she said to her husband, "but all that surrounds me seems decked with beautiful flowers." These were her last words. She immediately fell into a sleep, then died on October 25, 1555, at only twenty-nine years old. Though she died young, she had gained the fame, experience, and sorrows of a long lifetime. Protestants everywhere grieved her death.

The plague continued. Grunthler, dazed with grief, went everywhere in his doctor's work, recklessly exposing himself to the disease. He seemed to be courting death, and it came to him within a month. Emilio also fell victim. All three are buried in St. Peter's church at Heidelberg with this inscription:

> In the name of the eternal God and to the memory of Olympia Fulvia Morata, the beloved wife of Andreas Grunthler. Her remarkable attainments in several languages, the marvelous purity of her life and her piety elevate her above her sex. The witness of her life was even surpassed by that of her death. Peaceful, happy and holy she died in the year of our Lord MDLV., aged xxix. years, in a strange land. Here she lies with her husband and her brother Emilio.

Most of Olympia's writings burned up during the siege. Housework took over her time when she found safety. She did not live long enough to write anything new except letters. Her carefully educated brother died before he could really use his gifts, and she left no children. We could see Olympia's life as fruitless. But she encouraged

many Christians in her letters, and through her influence, someone
in the French court spoke up for the persecuted Huguenots. Some of
her writings survived and have been translated several times.[29] Today,
it is Olympia's example of faithfulness in a variety of difficult circumstances that stands as her greatest contribution to Christ's church. She
herself had written, "I long to be dissolved, so great is the confidence
of my mind, and to be with Christ in whom my life flourishes."[30]

---

29. The first collection of her works came out just three years after her death and
went through several republishings. The second edition is dedicated to Elizabeth I,
"patroness of the Christian church." Olympia Morata, *Olympiae Fulviae Moratae
Foeminae Doctissimae ac plane Divinae Orationes, Dialogi, Epistolae, Carmina, tam
Latina quam Graeca*, ed. Celio Secondo Curione (Basel: Perna, 1580), frontispiece,
dedication.

30. "Olympiae Votum," in Morata, *Complete Works*, 183.

# CONCLUSION

As you read these stories, perhaps you identified with a particular woman. Maybe you could relate to Anna Reinhard's care for her family, or Jeanne d'Albret's estrangement from her husband, or perhaps Katherine Willoughby's quick wit resonated with you. Each of the women in this book has something to teach us; each gives us a different aspect of what selfless service looks like. The lives in these brief biographies can encourage us in our daily work to be faithful with what God has given us where He has put us. Varied examples of Christian living can teach us how to live our own lives. Though the setting and practice differed from woman to woman, the principles by which they functioned were the same. That means we can also use them. Here are seven things common to the women we have discussed that would strengthen the church today.

First, a radical change in circumstances did not stop fruitfulness. These women often saw huge reversals in their lives: from Roman Catholic nun to Reformer's wife; from happily married to impoverished widow; from queen to fugitive; from provider to persecuted—these are changes that would shake anyone. But their situations did not prevent these women from being faithful and bearing fruit. Circumstance is just that: the situation that we happen to be in. It does channel and direct, but it does not define or dictate. Going from one stage or position in life for these women did not mean that they stopped their life's work. It meant that they had to reassess what their work was in their new circumstance. If they could continue their former work—educating children, writing to pastors, caring for husbands—then they did. If they could not because of a loss of position, money, freedom, or something else, then they reoriented themselves to a new calling. When Olympia Morata fled her home, she did not wait until she had her former life back in order to be productive; she continued writing and used her learning to teach her brother. When Anna Adlischweiler had enemy soldiers quartered in her home, she did not wait for a Protestant army to rescue her; she escaped to find her exiled husband. Thinking and acting as though our circumstances control us stunts our fruitfulness. Clearly, circumstances affect and can change our work, but they should never prevent us from faithful use of our gifts in some way.

Second, these women all had a multifaceted identity. Though they would not have thought about identity in the same way we do, we can see through their writings and their work that they thought of themselves primarily as Reformed believers. Perhaps it was this lack of labels that allowed them to be so many things at once. In the church today, women often think of themselves as "single working woman" or "homeschool mom" or "empty nester." This labeling is partly just a way of letting others know what our lives are like—what stage we are at and how we handle it—but it is also partly a default identity. It can be a way of staying inside our comfort zone by limiting ourselves to one or two particular identities, instead of leaving ourselves open and serving where we can. If we think of ourselves as "wife" and then are widowed, or we think in terms of our work and find ourselves laid off, it can cause an identity crisis. Often, if our self-appointed identity evaporates, our feelings of security and usefulness shrivel. When we think about how the women in this book had the versatility to be fruitful in many different situations, it is clear why they did not associate with one identity other than a spiritual one. They were Christians. They were Christians who served as many things at once: wife, mother, queen, author, hostess, leader, teacher. If one of those lesser identities was removed, it was replaced with another: wife to mentor, evangelist to correspondent. A sensitivity to providential directives and a trust that can translate to new circumstances mark many in the cloud of witnesses. If, as Christian women, faith is *the* identifying mark in our lives, then the shift of other roles and identities will not stop our fruitfulness; it will simply redirect it. A change of label will not shake us because we have a constant identity that cannot be changed. That does not mean that a change in how we think of ourselves is not hard; it was terribly difficult for Katharina Schütz to become childless after being a mother. But this does mean that when we think of ourselves as saved sinners bound for glory, merely serving in temporary capacities, we have the freedom to serve in many realms and also to let labels go when God removes them. An openness to any usefulness can be used powerfully.

Third, the Reformation women who were married to godly men knew that biblical headship and submission produce fruit. It is not something that squashes a woman's spiritual, intellectual, social, or relational abilities and opportunities. Instead, a marriage in which the husband leads in a Christlike way and the wife submits to that leadership has potential to change nations, as the good marriages in this book show. Katharina Schütz, "a little piece" of her husband, found encouragement from him to publish writings and serve the people of their city. William of Orange sought counsel and help from both his wives, whose advice could change history. Katherine Willoughby was enabled to protect and fund the church because of Brandon's position and means; Bertie encouraged and facilitated this work. One of the ways we can tell that the love of godly husbands strengthened instead of coddled or oppressed these women is how they dealt with widowhood; a good marriage equipped them for fruitfulness despite grief. Biblical partnerships helped make strong individuals, not weak dependents. Where husband and wife have the same goals and mutual respect, there can be loving leadership and trusting submission. When there is, both spouses will find encouragement, support, and freedom in their complementary callings.

Fourth, these women prove that good leadership is servanthood. Part of the reason that their leadership was so effective in their homes, churches, communities, and countries was because people could see them sacrificing comfort, time, and energy for others. People trusted their motives because there could be few selfish motives for what these women did. Multifaceted service gave them the right to lead in their sphere—in the dining room or in the throne room. Leaders who sacrifice for the good of those in their care can be trusted and followed into very unsettling situations, whether the followers are children fleeing with their mother or soldiers entering battle under the command of a princess. This is true for us. Is it clear that our service is not motivated by anything but a love for God and His church? Are we leading by serving in our homes, our churches, and our communities?

Fifth, everyone has gifts, and everyone needs to use them. The point is not whether we can feed dozens of refugees for weeks, write theological treatises, or lead armies. Each woman had gifts that she could use where God put her, and she used them. Margarethe Blaurer was no Olympia Morata, and that was fine; they each practiced their gifts in their own situations. Neither would have been able to substitute for the other. God used each exactly where He put them with the gifts He had given. Perhaps we are better at visiting widows in our congregations than we are at volunteering at a crisis pregnancy center, or vice versa. That is normal; the church is a diverse body, and each needs the other's gift. Are we using our gifts to the best of our abilities where God has placed us?

Sixth, God uses individuals' faithfulness to bring about His kingdom. Each woman discussed here had her faults. Some of them, like Louise de Coligny, had blind spots that the church could see when they could not. Some were too lenient; others were inflexible. A few made unwise choices that had deep effects. But each strove for faithfulness in life and doctrine, and God blessed it in different ways to different extents. Their work, which often facilitated or furthered their husbands' work, changed their families, communities, and even nations. Christianity that persistently welcomes the stranger, feeds the hungry, clothes the naked, and sacrifices self does not go unnoticed. Coupled with gospel proclamation, it is a saving testimony of grace. This is still true. It is faithfulness, not fame, power, or public displays of piety that the Lord values, rewards, and uses. God works through faithful believers who serve the church.

Last, death comes when our work is done, not before or after. Looking back, we can see each woman and her life's work in history's perspective. When Jeanne d'Albret died, the Huguenots mourned, not knowing that God was sparing her from unbearable grief. When young female martyrs had shortened lives, we can understand that their blood was the seed of the church. Those are things that can be difficult to see in the moment. But it is true for our lives too; the timing of deaths, including ours, might not make sense to us when they happen, but they will later. No Christian dies with unfinished work or extra time. When we have been sanctified and useful to the kingdom as far as God wants us, then we will go home. Not after, not before.

Why were these women able to live in these ways? How did these principles get lived out consistently over lifetimes? Perhaps perspective is the biggest reason. They thought in the long term; grace enabled them to see the big picture. Their goals were not a great weekend, or seeing kids through college, or even helping with grandchildren. Their goal, in different spheres, was the establishment and flourishing of a strong and faithful church that would be there long after they were gone. Because they were aiming for things beyond their life spans, it gave perspective and purpose to their everyday actions. Thinking long term gives us the ability to act meaningfully in the short term.

These women lived as they did because of sanctification: as selfless love replaced natural selfishness, they became fruitful. This sanctification was not a passive process. These women were not hanging out on social media or mommy blogs, waiting for spiritual maturity to happen. They actively pursued it: Bible reading, prayer, attendance at worship (often several times a week), fellowship with the saints, theological study and discussions, and conscious self-denial matured them into usefulness that God blessed. Personal projects, comfort, and plans were subservient to the mission of the Great Commission.

In fact, when we look at these women's lives in comparison with Scripture, we see a striking similarity between their examples and the directives in Hebrews 13. They continued in brotherly love, even though it was sometimes misdirected (v. 1). Sacrificial hospitality blessed their guests and families (v. 2). They visited or wrote to imprisoned believers (v. 3). Despite some unfaithful husbands, these women did hold marriage in honor (v. 4). Loss of property and wealth did not seem to shake them (v. 5). They certainly looked to the Lord as their ultimate and sometimes only help (v. 6). They occasionally struggled as people tried to lead them away by false teaching, but on her deathbed, each seems to have firmly trusted in Christ's sacrifice (vv. 7–12). Moves, exiles, and flight made it clear that they had no lasting city, but were seeking a heavenly one (v. 14). Their confessions of faith in the face of hostility were a sacrifice of praise to God (v. 15). This is simply conformity to the image of Christ.

Each woman had her own strength: intellectual, emotional, or physical. But spiritual strength was something they all had in common, drawn from a knowledge of the Scriptures and personal communion with God. It was conformity to God's Word that taught them how to live, how to offer their bodies as living sacrifices to their Redeemer. There is no such thing as superwoman. There is such a thing as an obedient, sanctified woman. In an array of talents, situations, personalities, tastes, and even blind spots, each woman bore kingdom fruit as each of their souls took on a biblical shape. The primary attribute that these women have in common is Christlikeness. Every believer has the same calling.

One of the amazing things about the cloud of witnesses is that it constantly grows. As we look back, we can see a part—the recorded part—of the large crowd. But strong, reforming women did not live only in the sixteenth century; they are there in the Old and New Testaments, and we can be sure that God is raising them up around the world today. We may not have heard of them yet, probably because many live in other countries. The women whom the church will write about in the future are living and working today. We just don't have their stories right now. Those stories will look different from the stories in this book because they are lived out in different times, places, and cultures—as far as I know, there is no Protestant princess leading a sizable army anywhere. But perhaps there is a pastor's wife in Nigeria who is sheltering refugees. Maybe there is a Christian businesswoman in China who is secretly distributing Bibles to places where they have not yet gone. There could be a believing wife married to a powerful, ungodly man in a developing country who is doing her best to teach her children the faith. Hopefully, our daughters and granddaughters will have their stories. Our job is to pray that God raises up women like this and that He equips us to be part of their number.

# APPENDIX A
## Time Line

c. 1484 — Anna Reinhard born

1492 — Marguerite de Navarre born

c. 1494 — Margarethe Blaurer born

c. 1497 — Katharina Schütz born

c. 1504 — Anna Adlischweiler born

1510 — Renee of Ferrara born

1517 — Luther nails the Ninety-Five Theses to the door of the church at Wittenberg

c. 1519 — Katherine Willoughby born

c. 1526 — Olympia Morata born

1528 — Jeanne d'Albret born

1534 — Act of Supremacy declares Henry VIII the head of the Church of England

1536 — John Calvin begins ministry in Geneva

1538 — Anna Reinhard dies

1541 — Margarethe Blaurer dies

c. 1546 — Charlotte de Bourbon born

1548 — Charlotte Arbaleste born

1549 — Marguerite de Navarre dies

1555 — Olympia Morata dies; Louise de Coligny born

1561 — Belgic Confession written

1562 — Katharina Schütz dies

1563 — Heidelberg Catechism written

1564 — Anna Adlischweiler dies

1566 — Second Helvetic Confession

1572 — Jeanne d'Albret dies; St. Bartholomew's Day Massacre

1575 — Renee of Ferrara dies

1580 — Katherine Willoughby dies

1582 — Charlotte de Bourbon dies

1598 — Edict of Nantes issued

1606 — Charlotte Arbaleste dies

1620 — Louise de Coligny dies

# APPENDIX B

## *Family Trees*

These family trees attempt to clarify often complicated family lines. For simplicity, they do not include every marriage or, with the exception of William of Orange's legitimate children, every birth. Dates are births and deaths. The children of Catherine de' Medici and Henri II are not in chronological order to show their daughter's marriage with Henri IV. Note that Catherine de' Medici is married to Jeanne d'Albret's cousin. Louis XII, Renee of Ferrara's father, married Mary Tudor after his second wife died. Katherine Willoughby is Lady Jane Grey's step-grandmother and survived the nine-day queen by almost thirty years.

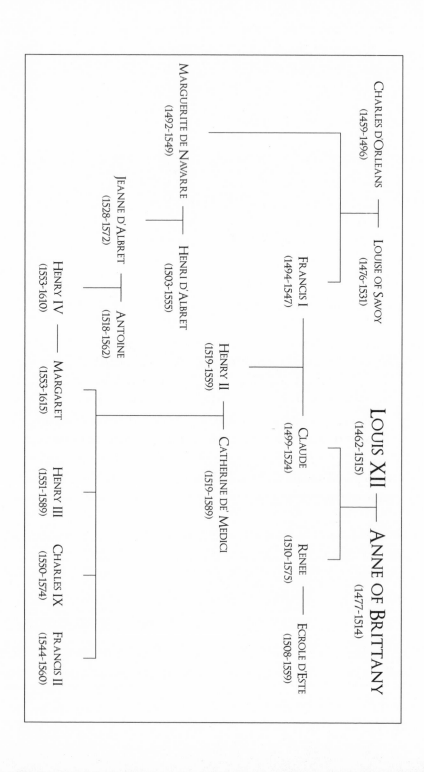

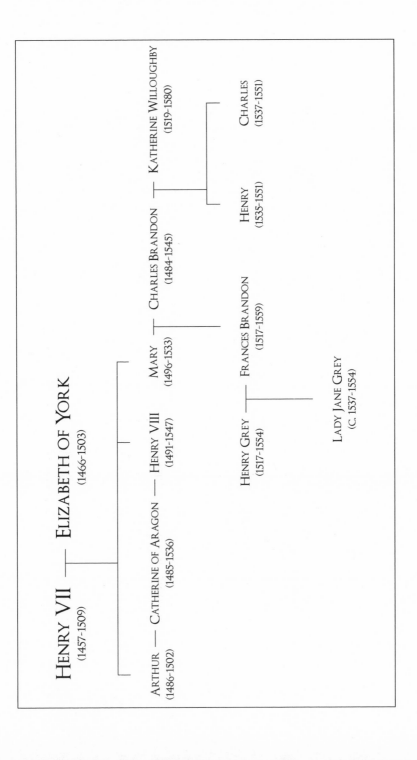

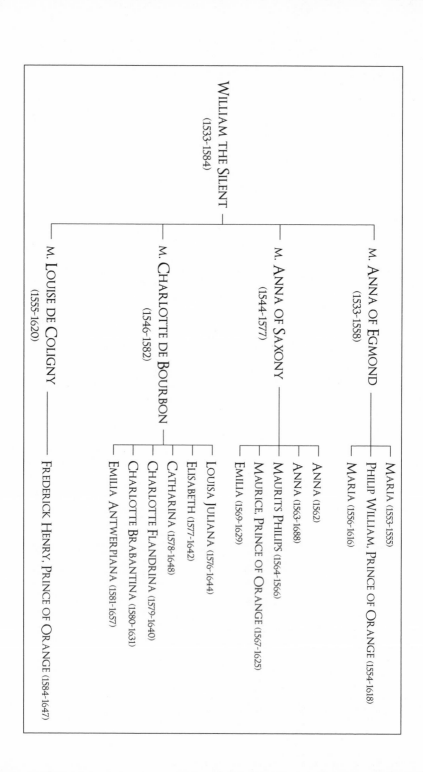

WILLIAM THE SILENT
(1533–1584)

M. ANNA OF EGMOND
(1533–1558)

MARIA (1553–1555)

PHILIP WILLIAM, PRINCE OF ORANGE (1554–1618)

MARIA (1556–1616)

M. ANNA OF SAXONY
(1544–1577)

ANNA (1562)

ANNA (1563–1688)

MAURITS PHILIPS (1564–1566)

MAURICE, PRINCE OF ORANGE (1567–1625)

EMILIA (1569–1629)

M. CHARLOTTE DE BOURBON
(1546–1582)

LOUISA JULIANA (1576–1644)

ELISABETH (1577–1642)

CATHARINA (1578–1648)

CHARLOTTE FLANDRINA (1579–1640)

CHARLOTTE BRABANTINA (1580–1631)

EMILIA ANTWERPIANA (1581–1657)

M. LOUISE DE COLIGNY
(1555–1620)

FREDERICK HENRY, PRINCE OF ORANGE (1584–1647)

# BIBLIOGRAPHY

Alexander, J. H. *Ladies of the Reformation*. Harpenden, U.K.: Gospel Standard Strict Baptist Trust, 1978.

Anderson, James. *Ladies of the Reformation*. London: Blackie and Son, 1858.

Bainton, Roland H. *Women of the Reformation: From Spain to Scandinavia*. Minneapolis: Augsburg, 1977.

_____. *Women of the Reformation in France and England*. Minneapolis: Fortress, 2007.

_____. *Women of the Reformation in Germany and Italy*. Minneapolis: Augsburg, 1971.

Baird, Henry M. *History of the Rise of the Huguenots of France*. Vol. 2. New York: Charles Scribner's Sons, 1900.

Barton, F. Whitefield. *Calvin and the Duchess*. Louisville, Ky.: Westminster John Knox Press, 1989.

Blarer, Ambrose, and Thomas Blarer. *Briefwechsel der Bruder Ambrosius und Thomas Blaurer, 1509–1548, Band III*. Stuttgart: Freiburg i. Br., 1910.

Bowles, Caroline. *Olympia Morata: Her Times, Life, and Writings, Arranged from Contemporary and Other Authorities*. London: Smith, Elder and Co., 1834.

Broomhall, Susan. *Women and Religion in Sixteenth-Century France*. New York: Palgrave MacMillan, 2006.

Bucer, Martin. *Martin Bucer Briefwechsel, Band III, Band V–VIII (1527–1529, 1530–1532)*. Leiden: Brill, 1995–2011.

Bullinger, Heinrich. *The Christen State of Matrimonye*. Translated by Miles Coverdale. Facsimile of 1541 edition. Amsterdam: Theatrum Orbis Terrarum, Ltd., 1974.

_____. *Heinrich Bullinger Diarium (Annales vitae) der Jahre 1504–1574*. Zurich: Theologische Buchhandlung Zürich, 1985.

Constant, G. *The Reformation in England: Edward VI, 1547–1553*. New York: Sheed and Ward, 1942.

Cook, Faith. *Lady Jane Grey: Nine Day Queen of England*. Darlington, U.K.: Evangelical Press, 2005.

D'Aubigne, J. H. Merle. *The Reformation in England*. Vol. 2. Edinburgh: Banner of Truth, 1994.

De Coligny, Louise. *Correspondance de Louise de Coligny Princesse d'Orange (1555–1620)*. 1887. Reprint, Geneve: Slatkine Reprints, 1970.

De Mornay, Charlotte. *Memoires de Madame de Mornay*. Paris: Jules Renouard, 1868.

De Navarre, Marguerite. *The Coach and the Triumph of the Lamb*. Translated by Hilda Dale. Exeter, U.K.: Elm Bank Publications, 1999.

_____. *Selected Writings*. Edited and translated by Rouben Cholakian and Mary Skemp. Chicago: University of Chicago Press, 2008.

Dentiere, Marie. *Epistle to Marguerite de Navarre and Preface to a Sermon by John Calvin*. Edited and translated by Mary B. McKinley. Chicago: University of Chicago Press, 2004.

Flemming, D. Hay. "Alexander Seaton." *The Original Secession Magazine* 17. Edinburgh: James Gemmell, 1886: 73–80.

Foxe, John. *Acts and Monuments of the Church…* New York: Robert Carter & Brothers, 1856.

Giselbrecht, Rebecca A. "Myths and Reality about Heinrich Bullinger's Wife Anna." *Zwingliana* 38 (2011): 53–66.

Goff, Cecilie Heathcote-Drummond-Willoughby. *A Woman of the Tudor Age*. London: John Murray, 1930.

Good, James Isaac. *Famous Women of the Reformed Church*. N.p.: Sunday School Board of the Reformed Church in the United States, 1901.

Gunn, Steven. *Charles Brandon: Henry VIII's Closest Friend*. The Hill Stroud, Gloucestershire: Amberley, 2015.

Hausser, Ludwig. *The Period of the Reformation, 1517–1648*. Edited by Wilhelm Oncken. Translated by G. Strange. New York: American Tract Society, 1873.

Higgs, Laquita M. *Godliness and Governance in Tudor Colchester*. Ann Arbor: University of Michigan Press, 1998.

Hone, Richard B. *Lives of Eminent Christians*. Vol. 2. London: John W. Parker, 1850.

Ives, Eric. *The Life and Death of Anne Boleyn*. Oxford: Blackwell Publishing, Ltd., 2004.

Kroker, Ernst. *The Mother of the Reformation: The Amazing Life and Story of Katherine Luther*. Translated by Mark E. DeGarmeaux. St. Louis: Concordia, 2013.

Marsh-Caldwell, Anne. *The Protestant Reformation in France: or, History of the Huguenots*. 2 vols. London: Richard Bentley, 1847.

McCrie, Thomas. *History of the Progress and Suppression of the Reformation in Italy in the Sixteenth Century*. Philadelphia: Presbyterian Board of Education, 1842.

McKee, Alise Anne. *Katharina Schütz Zell*. 2 vols. Leiden: Brill, 1999.

Morata, Olympia. *The Complete Writings of an Italian Heretic*. Edited and translated by Holt N. Parker. Chicago: University of Chicago Press, 2003.

———. *Olympiae Fulviae Moratae Foeminae Doctissimae ac plane Divinae Orationes, Dialogi, Epistolae, Carmina, tam Latina quam Graeca*. Edited by Celio Secondo Curione. Basel: Perna, 1580.

Morley, Henry. *Clement Marot and Other Studies*. London: Chapman and Hall, 1871.

Ridley, Jasper. *Bloody Mary's Martyrs: The Story of England's Terror.* New York: Carroll & Graf Publishers, 2001.

Roelker, Nancy Lyman. *Queen of Navarre: Jeanne d'Albret, 1528–1572.* Cambridge, Mass.: Harvard University Press, 1968.

Rolt, Richard. *Lives of the Principle Reformers, Both Englishmen and Foreigners, Comprehending the General History of the Reformation...* London: Bakewell and Parker, 1759.

Thysell, Carol. *The Pleasure of Discernment: Marguerite de Navarre as Theologian.* Oxford: Oxford University Press, 2000.

Van der Linden, David. *Experiencing Exile: Huguenot Refugees in the Dutch Republic, 1680–1700.* Farnham, U.K.: Ashgate, 2015.

Zell, Katharina Schütz. *Church Mother: The Writings of a Protestant Reformer in Sixteenth-Century Germany.* Translated by Elsie McKee. Chicago: University of Chicago Press, 2006.

Zwingli, Ulrich. *The Latin Works and the Correspondence of Huldreich Zwingli Together with Selections from His German Works.* Vol. 1, 1510–1522. Edited by Samuel Macauley Jackson. New York: G. P. Putnam's Sons, 1912.